PENGUIN BOOKS

The Gypsy Code

D1079602

The Gypsy Code

*The True Story of a Violent Game of Hide
and Seek at the Fringes of Society*

MIKE WOODHOUSE

PENGUIN BOOKS

PENGUIN BOOKS

UK | USA | Canada | Ireland | Australia
India | New Zealand | South Africa

Penguin Books is part of the Penguin Random House group of companies
whose addresses can be found at global.penguinrandomhouse.com.

First published 2019
004

Copyright © Mike Woodhouse 2019

Set in 12.5/14.75 pt Garamond MT Std
Typeset by Jouve (UK), Milton Keynes
Printed and bound in Great Britain by Clays Ltd, Elcograf S.p.A.

A CIP catalogue record for this book is available from the British Library

ISBN: 978-0-241-35724-8

www.greenpenguin.co.uk

For Jo C, empathy personified, with endless thanks for
your endless patience, and
Steve R, for breaking your moral code to help a friend
in need, thank you

October 2014

I opened my eyes to the pitch black of the caravan. It was the day of the funeral. Time to get up.

The bed filled the room completely, touching all four walls. To get out meant an awkward shuffle down and across to where I knew the door was. I paused for a moment, listening to Rhoda breathing beside me. Soft and gentle. An almost inaudible sighing. I moved carefully towards the door, trying not to wake her. She had a tough day ahead, we both did, and a few more moments of rest could only help.

Her grandfather, Riley, had been Gypsy royalty, and this afternoon we were going to bury him in a lavish Romany ceremony. Travellers from across the country would be joining his family at the graveside. As if paying respects to her grandfather wasn't enough, we had to cope with the fact that I'd be the lone gorgia, the Gypsy word for a non-Gypsy, in attendance. And I was a wanted man in some corners of the Traveller community, not that Rhoda knew it. But today was a day for grieving, not fighting. I hoped.

I popped the bedroom door open, off its magnetic catches, and the cold dawn light flooded in. Those flimsy trailer doors always felt like kitchen cupboards. Still, it was home. For now. And for Alfie, too, my great mass of loyal dog, standing there with his tail wagging back and forth.

I pushed open the door and he bounded off, scaring pigeons into the sky and pausing halfway down the plot to lift a leg. I always pissed in the hedge: no water supply meant the less we used the toilet inside the better. I tried not to think too hard about where I was living, on a patch of land next to a care home, and why I was there. A few years ago I'd had everything: a successful business, a Range Rover, a boat, and a wonderful home. I was a law-abiding and respected member of my community. Now I was living in a trailer on Gypsy land, and it would be cold in the caravan this winter.

Although the October dawn was beautiful, there was already a crispness to the air. And I felt sick with nerves about the funeral. When I heard the distant wail of a siren on its way to help some poor sod, I became very aware of the day ahead, and the nauseating taste of iron filled my mouth. I headed back inside.

We had a large commercial gas oven, more suited to a hotel kitchen than a trailer, and I lit three of the hobs to take off the morning chill.

'What's the time?' Rhoda called from the bedroom.

'Half six,' I replied, filling the kettle. 'How are you feeling?'

'I'm okay,' I heard, over the roaring gas rings.

When I poked my head into our bedroom all I could see was a dark mass of hair spread on the pillow.

'Fancy a cup of tea?'

She slid across the bed, bringing the duvet with her. I kissed her cheek, knowing the day of mourning would be hard for both of us. Rhoda had been Riley's favourite grandchild. Since we'd been in Essex he'd been over to visit us more than any other member of his large Gypsy family. He liked the way we were living in the trailer, no water, no electricity, a basic lifestyle he felt connected to and admired. Despite his age, he'd been a powerful presence, with lump-hammer hands that he'd used to fight anyone and anything his whole life. His affection for Rhoda was obvious, drawing inevitable friction with her cousins, who were jealous of his attention.

That was just one cause of our anxiety. Rhoda was fresh out of hospital the day before: she'd discharged herself, determined to attend her grandfather's funeral. Everybody knew of the special relationship they'd shared, and she'd be a focus of attention throughout the proceedings. Having a gorgia as a partner was yet another thing for her to deal with. Hundreds of travelling folk would be there from all over the east of England, and I'd stick out like a sore thumb.

I passed her the cup as she sat down, wrapping her dressing-gown tighter around herself. She'd been crying, I could see that, but she still had her natural beauty. Despite our ups and downs, she was always the woman who'd walked into a bar and entranced me from the moment I'd seen her.

Her perfect nails drummed an anxious beat on the cup. We sat and drank our tea. Alfie was barking at some birds that had landed on the trailer roof, their clawed feet hopping about on the thin aluminium. It had become a morning ritual, Alfie loudly announcing his freedom from the trailer, while the birds taunted him, safely out of reach.

'What do you want from the container?' I asked. Most of our clothes were in the forty-foot shipping container beside the trailer.

'Anything Karen Millen,' came the expected response. 'And black, obviously.'

I went back outside. The container hinges groaned as I swung open the heavy steel doors. Inside was all of my furniture from my house in Derbyshire. The pain had never healed from my forced departure. Every time I looked at a lifetime of possessions stacked in there because they wouldn't fit in the caravan, I'd think, how did it come to this?

I

Dawn. The alarm jackhammered through my head. I should be moving.

It was early November 2001. Even though I was the wrong side of thirty years old I still felt fit, despite the aches and pains from rugby training the night before. The autumn air had been cold, with clouds of exhaled breath from the players glowing in the floodlights and floating above the sodden training ground. I'd got through the practice fine . . . but I'd stayed at the clubhouse for a few pints with the lads. After a hard session on the pitch we'd recovered with a harder one at the bar. Those beers had felt good last night, but less so the next morning.

A swift cuppa later I was in the car and heading for the yard. I was working for a small engineering company, and had recently progressed from the business end of a welder into sales. I loved it. I liked the guys I worked with, and I believed in the product. I'd started my working life as an engineer but left when I was offered a well-paid residency as a DJ in a new Norwich nightclub. I spent years in the vacuous nightlife industry, as a DJ or running one of the busiest bars in the city, and my return to engineering was a real tonic. The contrast was stark yet welcome. Working in bars had been fun while it lasted, but it felt like hedonistic fooling around rather than investing time and effort in a serious career.

Now I was back in a 'real job', as my father would emphatically say. The company serviced the food industry, mostly chicken-processing plants. My working week had gone from twenty-five hours to sixty, and instead of chatting up girls, boozing, and entertaining crowds of drunken teens and twenty-somethings at a noise level that would damage my hearing, I was crawling through roof voids and under conveyor-belts. Thankfully my body clock had adjusted to getting up for work at the same ungodly hour I'd previously gone to bed.

As I pulled into the yard and parked, I saw a group of the lads standing outside the workshop, looking pretty pissed off about something.

'What's happened?' I asked Charlie, the foreman.

'Thieving bastards have nicked the tipper columns,' he snapped.

I knew how valuable they were, not just the price of the stainless-steel, but the work that had gone into them. We'd had to send them away to be processed by another company at great cost. The scrap value would be hundreds of pounds, but they'd cost us a small fortune. We all knew the pressure this would create, and there were deadlines with important customers waiting for the machines.

'Fuck's sake,' cursed one of the lads, kicking a bit of wood across the yard.

We'd suffered a run of thefts lately, including diesel,

heating oil and scrap metal. And we were all seething. I went into the office to find Paul, my boss, pacing back and forth.

'Morning, Mike,' he muttered, his face scarlet with rage.

Paul and I had a good working relationship, and though I often played the fool he knew that beneath the laughter I was a more-than-competent engineer. Most days I'd arrive in the office and lighten the atmosphere with a wild tale or a recently heard gag. This wasn't one of those days. I really felt for Paul: the theft would cause him massive problems as well as costing him a lot of money.

I was thinking about what I could do to take some of the pressure off him, and offered to phone the customers and explain the forced delays.

'I can visit some in person,' I suggested. 'Apologize face-to-face.' I also had a security idea that might stop the thefts. 'We need to vary our times in the yard. Let different lads leave their cars here and take a van home, keeping the lights on in the workshop. Make it harder for the thieves to guess if we're here or not.'

Paul nodded his approval. It was agreed that we'd take turns to come in as early as four in the morning and stay as late as ten. Some of the lads voiced justifiable concerns about what would happen if they disturbed a robbery. We'd all heard stories about how thieves could be violent if they saw the need, and our lads were engineers, not unpaid vigilantes. Still, there were enough of us happy to join in and try to deter the criminals. We also contracted a security firm to visit the yard at least twice a night at random times, and posted signs showing a fierce-looking Alsatian on the gate.

These measures seemed to work for a few weeks, and a couple of the lads reported hearing a vehicle pull into the yard, then running outside to see tail-lights disappearing down the lane.

Anyway, it was my turn to go in early so I was up at four and heading into work at half past. The yard was down a lane opposite the church, about a quarter of a mile outside the village. Typical of many rural villages that had suffered in the Great Plague, the houses that had once clustered around the church had been burnt down and the whole village had relocated up the road. The churches were too valuable to rebuild so now stood remote from the communities they served. I was driving one of the company vans, and my red Audi was parked in the yard. My first ever vehicle had been a van and I loved the elevated driving position. You could see so much more over the hedges, and as I drove along the lane a barn owl swooped over the meadows, patrolling the fields and hunting for breakfast.

He wasn't the only one looking for prey.

I pulled round the side of the main shed to park, and there they were, bold as brass: two thieving bastards in the skip, throwing stainless-steel offcuts and scrap into a pickup.

'Got you,' I said to myself, grinning as I slammed into reverse to try to block the gateway.

It's a mystery to me as to how they beat me to the gate,

but they did. Ugly faces stared at me as they sped past and up the lane. I slewed round on the concrete sugarbeet pad and gave chase. By the time they'd reached the church I was right behind them, and we both turned sharp left, heading into Redgrave. I scrabbled about on the seat for my phone, and dialled 999 as we shot past the pub at seventy miles an hour.

'I've caught them,' I shouted down the phone. 'Two of the thieving bastards.' The adrenalin had kicked in, and I was making no sense.

'Where are you and who have you caught?' came the calm response.

I knew who they were all right: two of the Smith clan, a local Traveller family. They were infamous for being behind almost every theft or petty crime in the area. By the time I'd explained who I was chasing, and where we were, we'd screeched through the village and reached the crossroads. They took a violent left, balancing their old banger on two wheels, the scrap metal shifting across the truck bed.

Time to concentrate on my driving. 'I'll call you back in a minute,' I hung up the phone, got two hands back on the wheel, and nearly hit them at the crossroads. I knew a tricky bend was coming up, especially at that speed, and sheet metal can have an almost liquid quality when it's loose, so I hung back as we approached the bend. This had to be timed just right. A hundred yards from the corner I floored the accelerator pedal.

I hit their bumper as their brake lights came on. Perfect.

Watching the pickup go off the road was almost a thing of beauty. They careered up the verge and smashed into the brick wall of a factory entrance.

I slammed on the brakes. Time stood still as I realized what I'd done. I could've killed them. Then they scrambled out of the wreckage and started jogging down the road. I wound down my window and drove beside them. 'No point in running, you wankers.' I laughed. 'I know exactly who you are.'

They jumped through a gap in the hedge and fled across the meadow. Suddenly the surge of adrenalin was overwhelming. I felt sick and euphoric at the same time. I reversed the van back to the factory entrance where a crowd of employees in white coats and blue hairnets had gathered around the mangled pickup. Steam poured from the crumpled bonnet, and I jumped out of the van, shouting, 'Yes! Yes! Fucking *yes*!' I pumped my fist in the air, confused onlookers staring at me. Who on earth would celebrate such an accident? A guy with an overdose of adrenalin coursing through his veins, that's who.

My plan had worked, and I'd been the one to catch them, not just to scare them away from the yard. I'd actually had the chance to take some revenge. They'd lost their pickup, and I wondered how many people had lost valued items to that very truck. Now it was a write-off. And I'd done it. I hadn't just run into the office and called the police: I'd seized the moment and dished out some justice. It was a high I'd never felt before. Every guy wonders what he might do when the chips are down, and I'd acted on impulse without a trace of hesitation or fear.

Laughing, I grabbed my phone and redialled the police. They were already on the way from my first call and arrived within minutes. I also called Paul and told him what had happened. He arrived with the police, looking as happy as I was. I posed for photographs with the wrecked pickup, my foot on the bumper, arms crossed, the crowd offering handshakes and congratulations. A stick-on banner across the top of the pickup's windscreen read: *Fuck work, let's party*.

Fuck work, let's go thieving, would've been more accurate.

Next a dog team turned up, and the handler asked me where exactly they'd gone through the hedge. I walked up the lane to show him as the dogs pulled on the leashes, barking in anticipation of the hunt. Two beautiful German shepherds, intelligent brown eyes and masses of exposed teeth ready to go.

'Can I come?' I asked, before I realized what I'd said. I think the chase had earned me some respect as the dog-handler nodded.

'Stay back at least twenty yards,' he instructed, 'and follow in my tracks. You can identify them when we catch up.'

I set off behind the dogs, jogging to keep up. I found out afterwards that they don't follow the scent of the prey, but the trail of disturbed pollen across the ground. They were on point and going fast. I was trying to work out how far ahead the thieves might be with a five-minute head start, but after about a mile we entered a farmyard and the ferocity of the dogs' barking increased. I followed the handler and the excited dogs into an open-fronted barn. Behind an old red tractor, trembling in the corner, were the two thieves.

'Come out and get on your knees,' the officer commanded. There was no argument or resistance. The dogs looked and sounded vicious. I was sure the handler would happily have unleashed them for some sport.

The commotion had drawn the owners of the property outside, an elderly couple, obviously coined up to the hilt. She was in her dressing-gown and slippers, head craning round to see whom the dogs were barking at, but keeping her distance. The man was already dressed head to toe in practical country green, from his wellies to his peaked cap.

'What's all this?' he asked the dog-handler, his voice almost drowned by the barking. A short command and the dogs sat down, suddenly quiet. 'What's all this, then?' the old boy repeated.

'Two suspects of a theft hiding in your barn,' replied the policeman.

He turned to me. 'Are these the two from the truck?'

They hadn't moved an inch. Two sorry-looking thieves on their knees. One of them had a bad cut on his hand, and I could see the blood dripping on to the concrete floor. Shame it wasn't his neck, I thought.

'Yes,' I confirmed. 'That's them, all right.' It was a strange moment, locking eyes with them again. The anger in their stares, but also fear. 'Couple of thieving pikeys.'

The dog-handler shot me a withering look. 'Pikey' was a derogatory term used to describe Travellers. Nobody knew the origins but it was the standard word of choice if you were on the other side. But the copper was trained to be neutral and his face made it clear that I shouldn't repeat it.

The men said nothing, paralysed by the threat of the dogs. After a brief chat the owners headed back indoors, armed with an exciting tale for the next village meeting or round of golf. A few minutes later the lady of the house reappeared with a tray of tea and biscuits, as if hosting an impromptu get-together. There were four cups on the tray, as she'd even made some for the thieves. How bizarre and quintessentially English, I thought. The policeman and I gratefully took our cups, and I was waiting for the Travellers to stand up and get their tea, but the dogs stood guard in front of them, daring them to move with steady eyes and low, grumbling snarls. The last two cups went cold, untouched on the tray. It was a surreal situation, but I couldn't stop grinning.

The dog-handler had already radioed in for assistance, giving the address and suspect details, and in short order two patrol cars pulled up to take the thieves away and return us to the factory.

I was buzzing as I drove back to the yard. The whole experience was racing on repeat through my head. Most of the guys offered back-slaps and high-fives, but a couple of the older heads voiced concerns: 'You don't mess with the Gypsies,' they said. They told a few tales of revenge attacks on folk who'd confronted them before. Beatings and arson. I laughed them off: I was too high to worry about that. After months of petty thefts, a strike back against them was long overdue, and I felt invincible.

2

A few weeks had passed since the theft from the yard. I'd heard a few wild tales about the Smiths being on the hunt for me, but I was staying in Botesdale, a small village a few miles away from Ledburgh, so I felt safe enough. Nobody knew where I lived, which meant they had two choices – turn up where I worked or at the rugby club. The thought of them rocking up at the rugby club made me laugh.

On the day of the theft I'd made a statement to the police, detailing what had happened. Even they'd warned me to be extra careful for a while. Who were this family to be regarded as so dangerous? I'd seen them around Ledburgh, shuffling along in their hoodies with dull expressions. Always in numbers, rarely on their own, and maybe that was their singular strength. On my visits to town I'd received nothing but handshakes and pats on the back from different folk who'd suffered at the hands of that family. Stories of theft, intimidation, drug-dealing, bullying, and even rumours of a gang rape. They were already the lowest form of scum in my eyes, and the stories just confirmed my feelings. I was being congratulated on taking a stand, and I was enjoying the attention.

I was constantly hearing tales about the Smiths and the trouble they caused in Ledburgh, and it was hardly surprising that most of my conversations at the time were dominated by my apparent heroics.

The bulk of the Smith clan lived in a street of council houses on the edge of town. Initially they had had just one property, but as neighbours were driven out they'd claimed the whole row. I heard how they'd knocked through the walls between the houses, so if the police turned up at one door they could escape out of another. The place was a disgrace. Piles of scrap metal, old washing-machines, any old rubbish they'd gathered, all was dumped in the front gardens. God knows what a state there was inside. People had even seen horses looking out of the windows, and one guy swore he'd seen one in an upstairs bedroom. The only thing that would fix that mess was a wrecking ball.

On Fridays after work a few of us would go down to the Redgrave Crosskeys, the pub I'd recently driven past at such high speed, for a few end-of-week drinks. I looked forward to those early-evening sessions: the pub was busy for a village boozer, and I enjoyed the company I was keeping. Paul was a regular, and we'd often put the world to rights over a few beers. This particular Friday, still on a high from catching the Smiths red-handed, I saw a very attractive girl hanging around the pool table. After a few pints of Dutch courage, I wandered over to say hello.

'Fancy a game of pool?'

She nodded, and I started racking up the balls.

'We could make it more interesting,' I said. 'If I win I'll take you out for some food.'

She smiled. 'And if I win?'

'I'll strip off and jump in the duck pond.'

Laughing, we shook hands and started the game. I needed to be on my best form: the duck pond was a miserable brown mess of stagnant water, encircled by mud and reeds, beside the road near the pub.

On my second shot, to my utter horror, the black rolled into the corner pocket. Laughter echoed around the pub. We all knew each other, and everyone had come to watch the frame unfold.

True to my word I stripped off on the village green. Covering my frontal dignity I walked into the pond. The smell was overpowering. A foot of water, then two feet of slime and duck shit. I stood in the middle posing for a photo, then made my mud-encrusted way back to the pub. Using some beer towels I got most of the filth off but the smell clung to every part of me.

'I'm Mike, nice to meet you.'

'I'm Sarah.' She was still in hysterics. 'My pleasure.'

'I deserve a rematch,' I claimed, pulling my shirt back over my head. 'Same terms.'

'A date or the duck pond?'

'You're on.'

Unfortunately the invincibility I felt after nabbing the thieving Smiths didn't stretch to the pool table. Sarah cleared up, and didn't even look at the black as she slotted it down. I'd been well and truly hustled. The pub was in uproar. Nobody could believe I was going back into the pond. But I did. If anything, it was worse because I'd stirred it all up on my first visit. I went home soon after for a hot shower, never securing a date with Sarah.

The photo of me standing naked in the pond went on display behind the bar for months. However, the fun of that night, the camaraderie of my community, was brought back to harsh reality a few days later when a police car pulled into the yard, and an officer walked over with a tight smile on his face.

He explained that a date had been set at Thetford Magistrates' Court for the end of the month. Paul confirmed he'd go with me, and had made a statement to the police about the series of thefts from the yard, and also his involvement on the day of the Smiths' arrest. The police told him he didn't have to attend, but he insisted on going. As well as wanting to support me, he hoped to see some justice served.

I was fine until the night before when the nerves kicked in. Was I doing the right thing? Paul had said it was okay if the charges were dropped, aware of the danger I was in. But no, my mind was made up. I wasn't giving in to threats or warnings of retribution.

On the morning of the court case we suited up and drove into Thetford. We parked at the other end of town in case there was any trouble – no point in risking vandalism to Paul's car – and walked towards the courthouse . . . where a reception party was waiting for us.

Seven members of the Smith family stood on the steps, all in different-coloured Adidas tracksuit bottoms and dirty trainers. Fear knotted in the pit of my stomach.

But at that point in my life I had a firm belief in justice and the justice system. We'd have our say in court or be damned. And a strange sense of bravado took over.

I'd played most of my rugby as a gobby scrum half, encouraging huge opposition players to pick up the ball and run at me. This attitude had often ended in regret, my head bouncing off their knees as they smashed me into the muddy pitch. But, like a yapping Jack Russell, I never seemed to learn.

I went into character, handing my jacket to Paul.

'What the hell?' Paul muttered, as I passed him my tie. He stood still as I strutted forward.

'Only seven of you?' I mocked. 'You really should've brought some help.' My heart was racing, white sparks flying in my eyes. Here we go, I thought, as they started to move down the steps, confidence in numbers. My fists were clenched, and I was debating whether to pose as a Queensberry Rules boxer, do the Ali shuffle, or just go full windmill.

The doors burst open and four policemen rushed out and split us up. They'd been watching from inside, and I realized they'd have been happy if we'd turned around and left the guys with no case to answer. I couldn't understand it. Anyway, they ushered us apart, and the showdown was settled with some hard stares but nothing more. I was relieved, and as we walked into the courthouse the colour returned to Paul's face.

'You mad idiot,' he said, a glint in his eyes.

The hearing was an absolute farce. I was warned

repeatedly for using the names of the accused during my testimony, to the point of being threatened with contempt of court if I persisted. So I started nodding in their direction. This warranted another warning. It was becoming painfully obvious that the court had no interest in pursuing a conviction. I voiced my frustration that I was being talked to in a sterner fashion than the suspects. This won me no friends on the Bench, and I could see where the outcome was heading.

Due to a lack of forensic evidence the magistrates concluded that the theft charge would be dropped, and that just a minor driving charge would be brought. I was furious. I'd put my head over the parapet, expecting some support, but the authorities had treated them as if they were untouchable. No wonder the Smiths felt they had a free hand to behave as they wished in Ledburgh. For years folk had suspected that they were snitches for the police, trading information on fellow Travellers for leniency. Rumours abounded about police raids on other Traveller sites, and also on regular businesses that had pushed their luck, bending a few rules to turn an extra pound. When anyone wondered where the police had gathered their information, suspicion had fallen time and time again on the Smiths. That made sense in the circus that had just taken place. Combine that with police officers, remote from the community they serve, having no understanding or interest in the plight of the townsfolk. With the departure of the local bobby, we'd become no more than faceless statistics, both criminals and victims.

The Smiths grinned as they left, kicking over a bin in the reception area. I stared hard at the magistrates sitting on the Bench. None of them would look me in the eye. We half expected the Smiths to be waiting outside, but it seemed they'd left without a backward glance.

'Well, that was a complete waste of time,' said Paul. He sounded resigned to the outcome. 'I can't believe what we just sat through. No wonder they feel they can just take anything they want, if that's how the courts deal with it.'

There was nothing I could say to change the truth. Those guys had a free pass. Even if you caught them red-handed they still walked free without sanction. They'd figured out there was only a slim chance of being caught, and even then a laughable possibility of conviction. Without a deterrent, the rewards of their crimes outstripped the risk. Something had to be done.

3

Rugby has always been a major part of my life. I've played since I was seven years old, starting off at North Walsham RFC, moving on to Norwich, then Ledburgh, a rural club built on the foundation of proud families that have farmed the area for generations. There's a special camaraderie in rugby due to the physical nature of the sport. This is a game where your teammates must protect you from actual bodily harm. Looking out for each other on the pitch binds players together, and I loved being part of that brotherhood, revelling in the talk at the club that, for a while, was of little else but my Gypsy hunting escapade.

Almost all of the local farmers had suffered at the hands of the Travelling community. There was nothing worse than a ragtag convoy of vehicles turning up on their land unannounced. Every farmer knew it meant a period of theft, damage and a huge mess to clear up afterwards. Debris from fake tree-surgery operations, rubbish clearance, all mixed with human waste would be spread around the area and left for someone else to clean up when they finally moved on.

A regular complaint from farmers at the club was the loss of red diesel. With the invention of battery-powered grinders most padlocks were useless, and if the locks became a problem the thieves simply drilled into the tank and drained the contents into containers. A story had gone round about the theft of two massive generators from Trinity Park in Ipswich. Each was the size of a twenty-foot shipping container, and protected by a security guard with two dogs. The robbers shot the dogs dead and beat the guard to within an inch of his life. The generators had trackers fitted so the police found them the next day, buried in pre-dug holes, covered with tarpaulin and a foot of soil. Next to a Travellers' camp.

With this vicious raid in mind, disturbing an ongoing theft was not the wisest option.

Another story often repeated was of how a huge bright yellow trailer had been stolen from a local farmer. He suspected it had been taken to a nearby camp so complained to the police, who'd declined to investigate in case it caused a riot. So the farmer got hold of his friend's light plane and flew over the camp for a look. Sure enough, there was his trailer. He made a few passes across the site, taking photos of both the trailer and the crowd of slack-jawed men shaking their fists at the plane. Armed with his photos, he returned to the police and demanded action. They had no choice but to go to the camp entrance and ask nicely if the trailer could be returned. It was wheeled out on to the road reluctantly, amid claims that some dodgy-looking guy had sold it to them the day before. They even asked for the money they'd supposedly spent on it to be compensated, as they were now the victims of crime.

These impromptu Traveller camps also brought frustration to the wider local community, who quickly became victims in the spate of burglaries and thefts from sheds and garages. Dogs were also stolen on a regular basis, either for breeding or fighting, and losing a cherished family pet to these folk was particularly painful. Stories were common of carcasses that had been found ripped to pieces and buried near abandoned camps, their faces still muzzled with duct tape so they couldn't offer even the least defence. The fighting dogs would be half starved, whipped into a frenzy, then unleashed on some terrified domestic pet. It was classed as training, preparation for the next big-money dog fight. The thought of a beloved pup's tormented last hours, snatched from its garden by strangers, bagged and thrown into a van, kicked and beaten, before some cruel bastard taped shut its mouth, tied it with a short chain to a stake driven into the ground, then let it loose for some other tortured beast to maul it to death made me feel sick. I'd even heard that some of the bodies had been discovered half eaten.

The beleaguered locals would feel it was partly the farmer's fault for letting the Travellers remain on their land, as if they were complicit in some way. The police were either powerless to help, or not interested. It was a lengthy and costly procedure to get Gypsies moved on, and was normally met with threats of violence or dire retribution, which weren't just hollow words. One of the lads I knew from playing rugby had lived near a Traveller site in London. He told me that when a local shopkeeper had kicked out a load of kids for stealing sweets one of the dads had come back with a crossbow and shot him through the shoulder. 'Not to mention the car they chased and set alight,' he added.

'Jeez!' I exclaimed. 'What on earth did they do to upset them?'

'Sped past the camp too fast. So they drove the bloke down and torched his motor.'

It was after a fairly heavy session at the rugby club that I was drawn into conversation with a local farmer. Ruddy-faced from years of outdoor work, and a few too many whiskies, he was suffering from just this predicament.

'I'm stuck, Mike,' he confessed. 'I've been on the phone to the police every day, and they keep saying there's nothing they can do.'

Six trailers, pulled by Transit vans and trucks, had set up camp on his estate. The field had no locked gate, so legally they'd been able to drive on to it. He'd gone down there and tried asking them to leave, and they'd told him to fuck off. Within days he'd lost items from the farm. Anything metal just disappeared. They'd tried to steal his red diesel but on that occasion the locks had defeated them.

And the mess they were making was apocalyptic. Piles of human and dog faeces all through the hedges, and heaps of rubbish everywhere. Rubbish that they'd been paid to take from folks' homes, including fridges, freezers, stuff with no scrap value. He told me how another group of Irish Travellers had gone round the local housing estates handing out flyers, promising to take away unwanted junk at a bargain price. Folk signed up – it was quicker than driving down to the tip or hanging about waiting for a council collection. A fiver here, a tenner there, and before long the Traveller's truck was heaped with old settees, mattresses and other rubbish. Less than a hundred yards from the estate, literally just round the corner, they'd simply tipped it off the back and driven away. The homeowners had to go and pick up the rubbish they'd just paid to have removed. The Travellers who had arrived on his land were operating a similar scam, and whatever crap they hadn't managed to lob into various hedgerows they'd just dumped on his farm.

And the sad fact was that Gypsies and farmers used to get along in that part of the country. My grandparents had told me about the traditional Romany folk who used to pass by every year. They'd arrive in their horse-drawn vardos, the traditional hooped carts, with the children from the surrounding villages running alongside. All the colourful wagons and the clothes they wore made them quite a sight. The main purpose of the visit was for the harvest – they came to add much-needed labour to gather in that year's crops. There were no tractors in those times, all heavy agricultural equipment was horse-drawn, and one thing the Romany excelled at was horses. They offered a skilled service to a busy farmer. They'd graft hard in the fields, wanting the farmers to ask them back the following year. Then, after the harvest and a simple handshake, along with a decent wage, the Gypsies would leave until the next picking season, each party relying on the other for a successful harvest.

Apart from their contribution to the local farming economy, the Gypsies also used to organize a sports day, setting up events like high jump, long jump and foot races. Prizes were given, and local lads looked forward to competing each year. And the Gypsies took on tasks like knife-sharpening and boot repairs, all undertaken for a few pennies. So, their visit was an eagerly anticipated annual event, not something to dread, as it is in our modern times, and especially now by my increasingly desperate farmer friend, whose life had been made a misery by his most recent Traveller camp.

I sympathized. I felt his anger and frustration. Why should those people be able to turn up and act in that way? Why wouldn't the local council or the police help him? He went on to tell me about half a dozen burglaries in the area. His neighbours were angry that the Travellers seemed able to stay on his land and terrorize them. They were all full of advice as to how to tackle them and move them on, so why wasn't he taking action? Why was he being so weak?

His neighbours were being unfair. I liked him, and I'd had a bellyful of beer so I offered to help. If he swore not to tell a soul, not his wife, family or dearest friend, I'd move them on.

'How can you do that?'

'Best you don't know.'

He looked me in the eye, then put out his hand. We

shook. I'd move on the Gypsies for an agreed fee of a thousand pounds cash.

I woke the next morning feeling sick, due to the alcohol and a sense of foreboding. What on earth had I agreed to do last night? Acting the big man after a few beers. Bloody idiot. I should've phoned him right then and made light of it, blamed the drink, and our shared anger about the camp, then called it off. What was I thinking?

But there was an ever-growing feeling of crusader-style justice inside me. The court case had shown the authorities to be gutless. This action could be the catalyst for reversing the tide of unaccounted-for crime. It would send a message that our area was out of bounds to Travellers, and that there was a price to pay for stealing from our community.

There was no way I could do anything on my own, and I immediately thought of my two best mates, Tommy and Jason. As close as brothers, we'd been through lots over the years and I trusted them completely. The key issue was secrecy. If this was going to happen nobody must ever know. Ever.

I called them and we arranged to meet at the Hunters Arms. There, we got a round of drinks and moved away from the bar, taking a quiet table in the corner of the pub. It was our usual watering hole, and we would arouse no suspicion if we were seen enjoying a pint and a chat.

'What's this all about then, Mike?' asked Tommy, looking quizzically at Jason for a clue.

'Right,' I began. 'I've got a job for you both, for all of us.' I went through my proposition in some detail. Petrol bombs. Disguises. A motorbike getaway.

When I'd finished they just sat there, dumbfounded, with shocked expressions.

'And?' I held out my hands, waiting for a reaction.

Tommy leant back in his chair, folding his arms.

'Are you serious?'

I'd been friends with Tommy since college, where I was studying Economics, Biology and English. We'd bonded over a season of superb underdog rugby, beating teams we should've lost to on paper. He was six foot of country muscle, scruffy dark hair, dark eyes and skin, and a constant favourite with pretty girls. The dictionary definition of 'confidence', he had a ready smile and was the life and soul of any party. He was also as hard as nails, which might come in handy for what I was planning.

'Yes.' I leant forward. 'I'm serious.'

'We creep through a hedge,' said Tommy, 'throw a petrol bomb and ride away?'

'If we do this right, it sends a strong message,' I added.

I explained that, with careful planning, it would be low risk. The camp was very close to a road junction. Choose the caravan carefully, one with no children, hit it on the side away from the door so anyone inside could get out. The caravans were not wooden, and probably wouldn't burn fast, or at all. Two of us, there to help each other if needed, would jump on to motorbikes and ride away into the night.

'As simple as that,' I said, finishing my speech and picking up my pint.

Jason and Tommy sat and stared as I drank.

Then Jason said, 'I'm in.'

Those were the first words he'd uttered all evening. Usually quiet, it was worth paying attention if he chose to speak. A few years back he'd walked into a pub I was running in Norwich and quickly become a firm friend. Solidly built, with short-cropped reddish hair turning silver at the temples, he took life seriously, and his expression showed it. He wasn't much taller than me, five foot ten at the most, but bigger around the chest and shoulders. He might be a white-collar kind of guy, but he loved the gym.

'Thieving bastards deserve a lesson.' And that was that. Jason said no more.

'Me too,' said Tommy, finishing off his pint.

We needed one more recruit, someone with a motor-bike. I had a fellow in mind, whom they both knew. It was agreed, and we shook hands solemnly. The money wasn't an incentive: it was about payback. Justice. We'd talked about the need for absolute secrecy. Any loose talk could result in jail time, and the prisons had a strong Traveller presence. We'd be in real trouble if we got caught.

'No sharing this with family,' I warned. 'No gossip with friends or partners. No mysterious Facebook posts.'

The atmosphere was tense as we saw the gravity of what we'd been planning. Hard stares all round. Then Tommy broke into a smile, and within moments we were all laughing. The euphoria of expected adrenalin was infectious.

The wheels were already in motion.

4

I drew up my initial attack strategy on Google Earth. I'd heard it was a great tool for burglars scoping out properties for a break-in, and it gave me a bird's-eye view of the area where the Gypsies were camped. Scrolling across my screen I could see access points, escape routes, and any hazards, like ditches or ponds. We'd be running in the dark with no lights, so the route had to be as clear as possible. I worked out we could use a hedgerow as cover for getting back to the bikes.

Plan hatched, I called the lads to go through my ideas. Will had joined us, a skinny guy with a quick temper but mad about motorbikes and trustworthy. We sat in my cottage at Botesdale and, with my laptop on the kitchen table, I went over every tiny detail of the raid, and explained my reasoning for each action.

The other lads had been aware of the purpose of the meeting for almost a week, but all of this was new to Will. His shocked face was a picture as we all sat calmly talking through the raid.

'Jeez, Mike.' Tommy laughed. 'You should've joined the army.'

I laughed, too. Tommy's little joke had eased the stiff atmosphere for which I was grateful. 'If we stick to this, we'll all get away safe and sound.' I finally turned to Will. 'Are you up for it, mate?'

His belief in our group of friends was total. He'd known all of us long enough to trust that we were solid guys and would always watch each other's backs, no matter what might happen.

Will shook his head. 'You lot never cease to amaze me.' Then he grinned. 'I'm going to regret this one day but, yes, I'm in.'

Will had confirmed what I'd hoped to hear. The team was complete. We spent another hour going through and rechecking details, until all of us were happy that nothing had been missed. It was simple, direct. We picked up our beers and toasted the plan.

There was one last thing I had to prepare. The petrol bombs. They sound easy in principle, and on the news, as a child, I'd seen plenty of flaming bottles soaring towards army Land Rovers during the Irish Troubles. This was different. These had to work first time as there would be only one chance. And they also had to be safe in the rucksacks riding out there. Last thing any of us needed was a ball of fire on the back of a motorbike.

I got together a selection of milk, beer and wine bottles, half a dozen different types of cloth, and a few litres of unleaded petrol. The hardest part was finding a site to do the tests. The more I thought over the problems, the more risks I worried about. The risk of being seen and questioned. The risk of setting fire to myself if the bottle exploded in my hand. But I knew I had no choice but to get started: the clock was ticking.

For the test site I drove out to an old gravel pit, long abandoned and overgrown, scattered with a few bits of abandoned plant. Kids had smashed all the windows and the paint had long gone, a few patches of faded yellow breaking up the rust.

I parked and got out of my car. It was near dusk. Total silence apart from my own breathing. After a quarter-of-a-mile walk up the entrance lane I was pretty sure I was on my own. The gates were heavily padlocked, and I scaled a six-foot mesh fence to get access.

First I filled a milk bottle two-thirds with petrol, then tore up an old pillowcase and twisted a piece into a strip. I poured some petrol on to the fabric and forced it down the bottle neck. There was about six inches of soaked cotton left hanging out. Tripping over beside a lit fire bomb was not on my agenda, and I checked behind me to make sure I had a clear getaway. I pulled out one of half a dozen lighters I'd brought along and flicked my thumb over the mechanism. The fume-laden rag burst into flame and I turned and ran. I'd stood the bottle on the flat mudguard of an old dumper, and got about thirty yards away at a full sprint before the bottle exploded. Less than five seconds. I turned and watched the orange flare emit a plume of black smoke into the early-evening sky.

'That's not long enough,' I said aloud. 'Too dangerous.'

Once the flames had died away, I had another theory to test. The neck of a wine bottle was a lot longer than that of the milk bottle. With no air in the neck, the flame couldn't reach the petrol until the bottle was broken. My second twisted piece of pillowcase was stuffed into the slender neck of a green Sauvignon-Blanc bottle. Again, a sudden flame as the rag was lit, before I ran. I reached the same spot and turned to watch. The rag was still burning but the bottle just sat there. And sat there. Over a minute passed and the rag stopped burning. I waited a few more minutes before slowly approaching the bottle. I had one hand up near my face, ready to flinch and shield my eyes if anything happened. The charred remains of the rag were lightly smoking from inside the glass neck, which was warm to touch but seemed safe enough.

Well, that had proved the point. Wine bottles should be safe enough to hold, light, then throw, the glass smashing on impact. We needed wine bottles if we wanted to keep our hands intact. I prepared four more and took them about thirty feet from the old dumper. I stood them well away from each other and held the first. I lit the rag and instantly held the bottle at arm's length, the flame whipping violently in the air. I kept hold of the bottle, and a cold sweat ran into my eyes despite the heat from the burning rag. Counting to five had never taken so long in my life. Finally I threw and watched it arc through the air. The heavy base of the bottle hit the dumper with a dull clunk. Then breaking glass, and a whoosh as the rag ignited and released the petrol. I was transfixed. It was a work of art. Half the dumper was aflame now, a cloud of black smoke mushrooming into the air. I checked round the edge of the pit, searching the dusk for signs of any watchers drawn by the noise and the light from the flames. There was no one, thankfully.

I lit and released the other three petrol bombs in quick succession. One had looked as though the rag had gone out in flight but the existing flames had set off the petrol. So I had my design, tried and tested. Throwing two would increase the chances of success. I went home with a grim smile, reeking of petrol and smoke.

A few days later I drove past the camp to check that the layout of the fields was as shown on Google Earth. Something as simple as a new barbed-wire fence could bring disaster on the night. I parked half a mile away on a small lane and walked back towards the Travellers' site. I didn't try to hide – it would have looked very odd to be caught watching them. Instead I'd decided to wander past as if I were a rambler.

The track was perfect for our getaway. Thick hedge offered cover right up to the caravans, and the road surface was good enough for the bikes. As I walked nearer I could hear voices. Women were calling to each other across the camp in thick Irish accents. I'd reached a gap in the hedge, the nearest point where the lane ran by the camp. I couldn't see anyone outside the caravans despite the voices I'd heard, so I stood for a while looking through the gap. There were five caravans in a rough line, all decorated with chrome and those funny windows that stand out proud on the trailer side. Only a couple of vans remained, and I guessed the others were out working, or more likely nicking stuff. I earmarked the caravan on the left, gauged the distance and the direction from the hedge, then walked back down the lane and went home.

As I drove I went through the plan step by step, thinking through anything that could go wrong. I was happy enough. Then again, I was thinking just a few days ahead, rather than years.

The night was drawing near. We'd agreed to meet as few times as possible before the attack. And when we did communicate it was to be verbal, face to face, never by text or voicemail.

The bikes had been checked and rechecked. One breakdown and we'd be stranded at the mercy of Gypsies whose caravans we'd just torched. Tommy and I had outfits of old gear bagged up and ready, as I'd ordered all our clothes to be burnt afterwards. Not one piece of evidence must remain. I'd done a final drive-by the day before, and everything was exactly as we expected.

On the night it was all nervous energy between me and Tommy. We'd bought everything from charity shops in Thetford, clothes with zero traceability. At my house we'd dressed in the disposable clobber for the attack, and when we saw each other's outfits and realized we looked just like Travellers, we burst out laughing.

Then the bikes pulled up outside, and the joking stopped. It was time. We walked down the path towards the two bikes idling near the pavement. Jason was instantly recognizable, his thick frame sitting astride his monster of a machine.

On the second was Will, my first choice as the final member of the team. An old colleague from Norwich, over the years he'd shown he could be trusted when discretion was needed. That was my main priority. What we'd agreed to do could land us all in deep trouble. If we were caught it was either prison, or a vicious beating from a load of Gypsies. Will also happened to be an awesome rider. He was as skinny as a rake and I couldn't imagine how he handled his bike as well as he did, but he had a cabinet full of shiny trophies from his track days at Snetterton Circuit. Long brown hair poked out of his helmet, and he simply nodded as we approached. Tommy climbed on behind him, dwarfing him on the raised pillion seat. I tried to get my arms round Jason but gave up and reached behind for the pillion bar.

Then we revved away. It was only a few miles to the site, and the ride seemed to flash by. Half a mile from the camp we throttled down and coasted, approaching quietly and slowly. It was just gone midnight, but there were still a few lights on in the caravans. Finally Will and Jason killed the engines. The sudden silence was deafening.

This was the most dangerous part of the operation. If anybody had heard the bikes approaching, then go silent, it would arouse their curiosity at the very least. We all stayed still, quiet in the dark. If we were confronted, the plan was to say we'd stopped for a piss. Three long minutes dragged past – they seemed like twenty. Then

Tommy and I carefully took off our small rucksacks, reaching inside to pull out glass bottles two-thirds full of petrol, the pre-soaked rags stuffed tightly down into the fuel. The smell was heady. We looked at each other, no need for words. It was summer, but the air felt cold on my face. My stomach was knotted with nerves, and a taste of bile crept into my mouth. I spat, conscious of any noise. I'd decided against keeping the helmets on: we needed to hear and see everything. Which now included Tommy's breathing. And my own. I'd been told years ago to silence your breathing by opening your mouth as wide as possible. I probably looked like a lunatic, but it worked.

We darted across the field to the gap in the hedge. The nearest caravan was clearly visible in the twilight, the ghostly pale aluminium side interrupted by two small windows of darkness. I knew it from my surveillance trips over the last few days. The idea was to frighten these people, not risk anyone's lives. And certainly no children. I'd watched the camp enough to be satisfied that this trailer had a single adult occupant.

Tommy and I stood there looking at each other. Lighters ready. With a nervous strike we lit the rags. We both had gloves on, and had carefully wiped the bottles clean as I'd heard that police forensics could lift a partial fingerprint off broken glass.

Next thing I saw, Tommy's bottle was sailing through the air. I threw, and watched mine arc towards the caravan. It was hideous and transfixing. Beautiful and frightening.

Tommy had gone, turning away as soon as he released his bottle. I couldn't move. The noise of the double impact was deafening. Like both barrels of a shotgun. Then the night sky was ablaze as the whoosh of flame engulfed the side of the trailer.

'Move,' my brain screamed. 'Move now.' But my legs refused. It felt like I was detached, watching a film in slow motion. Then suddenly the film caught up and my senses were overwhelmed with noise, heat from the flames, and the tang of petrol.

I ran, sprinting hard for the gap in the hedge, then a sharp turn up the lane. Both bikes were running, and Tommy swung his leg over the pillion behind Will.

I was a good thirty yards behind. 'Get a fucking shake on,' Jason shouted, and I did. I jumped on the bike as Will accelerated away, the single-track lane suddenly lit up by his full beam. It had been long abandoned by the council, and was dotted with lethal potholes and patches of grass along the centre.

Jason wrenched back the throttle and we tore away, the front wheel lifting through four rapid gear changes. The engines screamed like chainsaws through the night. I'd urged both the lads to ride carefully, but that was soon forgotten. It was all I could do to hang on, and I tucked my head into Jason's back as trees whipped past. Within a minute we reached the junction where we'd planned to part ways, confusing anyone in pursuit, and looping out on two separate circular routes before rendezvousing at the meeting place. I watched Tommy and Will swing left, riding steadier now. Tommy glanced back and gave me a thumbs-up. We turned right and pulled away, throttling up to eighty within a few hundred yards. I squeezed Jason and shouted, 'Slow down.' I'd got the shakes. My legs, arms and hands were trembling uncontrollably. I couldn't stop them. I have no idea what Jason thought I was doing behind him. My jaw was clenched tight enough to shatter teeth, and my head was spinning.

It was pure adrenalin. Lots of people talk big about doing daring things, but very few follow through. We'd done it. Actually done it. I hadn't felt this high since my dad had taken me poaching as a child. We'd creep through the woods looking for roosting pheasants, armed with a torch and an air rifle. He'd told us that if we heard the keepers coming we should drag our boots across the ground and throw the rifle into the undergrowth, then run, looking upwards to follow the break in the trees to stay on the path. The mark in the ground would allow you to collect your gun early the next morning, and the slightly lighter night sky would keep you on the path in the dark. As a young lad this type of adventure was exhilarating, and I now knew how much I'd missed it.

Anyway, I hung on to the back of the bike until we arrived at the meeting place, a deserted garage forecourt. We rode in from different directions within a minute of each other. With the helmets on it had been impossible to speak or otherwise communicate, and once we'd removed them there was a pregnant pause. Then Tommy was laughing.

'Fuck's sake, Tommy,' I said, then joined in. Jason and

41

Will looked around until the laughter swept them away. We were all aware it was nervous laughter, the relief of escape, a come-down after the adrenalin. Whatever it was it felt good, and we hugged each other, bound by an uncommon tie that could never be undone.

'Why were you so far behind?' Will asked.

'I thought you were roasting marshmallows,' Tommy added.

'I was too scared to run,' I admitted. 'I froze.' It was a confession, and they all paused. 'What we've just done is serious.' I looked at each of them in turn. 'If anybody finds out we'll be in serious shit. Beyond anything we might imagine.'

The atmosphere was tense again, all of us thinking the worst. But I needed that realization to sink in. 'I know I don't have to say it again, but this secret dies with us.'

'Agreed,' said Jason, on behalf of everyone, I hoped.

'And don't forget to burn everything,' I reminded Tommy. 'Gloves, pants, trainers, everything.'

He nodded and remounted behind Will. Time to go. A couple of pats on the arm and both bikes roared into life, the noise suddenly deafening.

We'd done it: the first salvo had been fired. And there was no way I could've known what would be the final outcome.

5

A few days later I met the farmer at a local pub. His face was as serious as I felt. I'd been through a roller-coaster of emotions – guilt, fear, and also a strange sense of euphoria.

We sat down at a corner table, and over a pint the farmer quietly explained how he'd been questioned by the police. A passing car had seen the blazing caravan and called the fire brigade. The Travellers hadn't.

'What do you mean they didn't call?'

'Not a word.' The farmer shook his head. 'For some reason the police made a point of telling me that the Travellers didn't report the fire. And they wouldn't talk to them about what had happened. They just moved on without making a fuss.'

A cold sensation crept into my guts. Why, if your caravan had just been set on fire, would you not talk to the police? We guessed that the caravan had probably been stolen in the first place and an official complaint might invite unwelcome scrutiny. But it left an unspoken threat of revenge, and I could see that the farmer felt the same fear. The officers had made clear that they thought he knew more than he was saying, which was nothing, but he knew they didn't have any enthusiasm to pursue their enquiries. I guessed that the Travellers leaving could only be good news for the local police. What energy would they have to hunt down the vigilante who'd moved them on?

We talked for a while about other things, even drifted into social topics, as if by not discussing the fire it would diminish the impact of what we'd done. I left feeling happier, and he certainly looked it. Mutual assurances were made on lifelong secrecy, and as long as we stuck to that pledge, nothing could happen.

How wrong we were.

Before leaving the pub he handed over the promised cash. A grand in my pocket. The lads and I were booked in for a curry in Norwich, and I'd share it out there. I was looking forward to a good night out, paid for by our actions. Nobody had got hurt, nobody had got caught. The Travellers had moved on and things would return to normal.

Although the farmer did have a mess to clear up. The fire-damaged caravan, and all the debris of the site, was buried discreetly in his landfill, hidden on the estate. It was all cleared within a day, and hopefully nobody would even remember it within a few weeks. The police had suspicions about the farmer's involvement, but we'd agreed to stay away from each other for six months, no texts or calls, as mobile-phone records could be checked. These were simple precautions that made us both feel safer in case there was a formal investigation.

As time passed I felt more and more positive about the whole experience. It had worked so well I could see no reason why it wouldn't work again. It was right that communities fought their own corner, and this was the only language the Gypsies seemed to understand.

After all the excitement and the illicit thrill of the attack, going back to my day job was a drag. I wasn't enjoying my work. I was the highest-selling but lowest-paid member of the sales team, and my sales manager was a complete prick. How Paul had employed and promoted him was a mystery to us all. He was four foot six of incompetence. After the Piper Alpha disaster, a system of engineering traceability had been rolled out in the oil and gas industry. People had lost their lives, and it made absolute sense. But it also meant that an army of consultants and bureaucrats was looking for work. The government, in its eternal wisdom, implemented the programme into general engineering. It was a con, a farce, but there was money to be made. And, as my manager couldn't have sold ice cream on a hot summer's day, he jumped on the bandwagon, initiating a series of meetings about future meetings that made my eyes bleed.

One of the directors, my good friend John Reid, had just had a second stroke and was on sick leave. On days when I was based in the yard we'd have a cup of tea together and chew things over. He'd forgotten ten times the amount of engineering knowledge others could ever dream of learning, and I had total respect for his words of advice. He was also a great sailor, one of his many passions in life, and I used to crew for him at regattas on Wroxham Broad.

A chain-smoker, he'd hold the rudder with his foot while he rolled a fresh cigarette on a long tack across the water. Once during a race he dropped the lit end of the fag inside his shirt and burnt his chest, and in the ensuing panic he released the rudder, swinging the jib round to knock me clean out of the boat. We still came second.

John shared my opinion on most things, and I missed him at work. The company put him on statutory sick pay, despite his years of service, and left him to it. I was appalled: John had set up the firm forty years before and they had discarded him like a cheap suit. It was time to move on. Job and house. I'd seen many people unhappy in their work yet remain at the firm, trapped by debt, or just lack of confidence that it was possible to move on. All of my life I'd been fortunate enough to believe in myself, and it was around this time that I was working away from home and had a dispute over returning one weekend to play rugby. My boss commented it was a shame but I'd have to miss the game. Sod that. I left the site and played, handing in my notice on the Monday morning. My stint at that company was coming to an end. I just needed to reduce my outgoings, and then I could go for good.

Some of the players at Ledburgh RFC lived in a shared farmhouse, which was affectionately known as the Chateau. It was a huge old Suffolk pile, owned by Mark, a stalwart of the club. He lived in one end and the bulk of the building was rented out to his rugby friends. To move in you had to be selected by the existing residents, and host a meal there, hitting the standard with both food and alcohol. One of the guys was moving out and I was invited to throw my hat into the ring. My dinner at the Chateau must have been up to scratch: enough booze was consumed that I can't remember much about it, but within a few weeks I'd moved in.

Living there was the closest I can imagine to what an American frat house is like. Constant laughter, always people coming and going, endless parties or invitations to parties elsewhere. We'd all sit in the living room and surf the music channels. If you landed on a video with good-looking girls in it, everyone else had to drink. If you landed on a boy band, you had to finish your drink and pass on the remote. It was childish drunken behaviour but great fun. There was also a weird room upstairs with no windows, just big enough for a single mattress. Thrown on the mattress was a selection of old blankets and a couple of pillows. It stank. But it was an initiation, a rite of passage, for young players from Ledburgh to spend the night there. It was grim with the door shut, which was one of the conditions, but it was on the bucket list for any young player trying to be accepted in to the club.

Eating there was always a challenge: shared kitchens are a nightmare at the best of times. This took filth to a new level, with teetering piles of plates and dishes, and stinking bins that no one ever emptied. I came home once to find one of the housemates grumbling about the failure of his new diet attempts. Large, as he was affectionately known, was twenty-three stone of front-row forward and trying to shed some weight to get playing again.

'Bloody diet shakes are a waste of money,' he complained angrily.

'Not working?'

He'd recently invested in a huge quantity, much to the amusement of the housemates.

'I've gained nearly a stone in a week.'

Sitting beside a huge pizza was a pint of strawberry-flavoured shake.

'You're meant to have them instead of food, not as well as, you bloody idiot.' He'd been eating as normal, but adding the calorie intake of the shakes. I'm sure I remember seeing those tubs of powder in the bin later that day. Those were good times.

It was also a low-cost lifestyle. The rent was so cheap I felt I could risk leaving my job to start up a business on my own. With John's forced early retirement the heart had gone out of the firm. I had the contacts and now the opportunity, and I registered my own company, Saracen UK. I think my boss had expected my resignation, and as my relationship with my line manager had become so fractious, it was probably a relief. I told him as I left that if our paths ever crossed again I'd knock him out. And, at the time, I meant it.

I now had a new home and a new business. I started my company with a desktop computer in the corner of my room, and a mobile phone. Within days I'd set up meetings all over the country. I had limited funds so I called various friends living in Lancashire, Derbyshire and Wales to arrange digs with them to save on hotel bills. I sold my first conveyor system to a meat plant near Lancaster, and the profit was enough to run my operation for two years. It seemed I couldn't go wrong. This was the best time of my life. Again, I felt invigorated and invincible.

I met an old colleague for a drink, Rick Elvin, a six-foot-four kick-boxer, who could solve most engineering problems. People liked him, and we were a good mix, but Rick was a family man: he had a house with a mortgage, a wife and two daughters. For him to take a leap of faith was not as easy as it had been for me, and I worked hard to convince him the wages would be there. Work was rolling in and the business was growing fast, too fast for me to cope on my own, so I took a chance. I went and bought two brand new crew cab trucks, had them branded with the Saracen UK logo, then drove one to his house and gave him the keys. Rick loved cars and a new truck was enough to tip the scales. We shook hands, hit the road and started selling.

Rick had a real hands-on approach to sales: if a customer had an issue with a machine Rick would climb underneath it, quite happy to get covered with muck to fix any problems. With Rick on board we soon had a dozen contractors working every weekend all over Ireland, Scotland and locally in East Anglia.

I had no time to dwell on the Travellers, the motorbikes and the petrol bombs. Six months passed quickly, and I was surprised to come home one night and find the farmer sitting in his car outside my house.

6

I grabbed my jacket and we went for a walk. The land around the Chateau was beautiful: rolling meadows edged with thick hedgerows, full of birds and offering shelter for rabbits and hares. It was on days like this that I missed having a dog, although the farmer and I were hardly out on a country ramble. We had business to attend to, something serious, and we kept our own counsel for the first hundred yards.

'How are things going?' I asked, breaking the silence.

We hadn't spoken since that evening in the pub six months before. The idea had been that the less time we were seen in cahoots, the less chance there was of folk putting two and two together, then linking the petrol bombs and caravan burning to me and the farmer.

'Very good,' he replied. 'Very good.' He had this amusing habit of repeating the first words of a conversation. 'You boys all okay?'

I knew he was referring to Tommy, Jason and Will. He didn't know their names, and had never asked. I nodded.

'Have any of you heard anything?'

'Not a word,' I assured. 'As if it never happened.'

'Good, good.'

There was a distinct chill in the air, despite the

late-afternoon sunshine. I was glad of the jacket. He was wearing a typical farmer's checked shirt with the sleeves rolled up, seemingly immune to the dipping temperature. I could see he obviously had something troubling on his mind.

'Have you had any comeback at all?' I asked, pausing to turn and face him.

He laughed nervously. 'It took months for my nearest friends to believe I'd played no part in moving them on.' He explained that lying to everyone had taken its toll on him. Some of his closest friends had pressed him to confess that he knew more than he admitted. 'That's why it's so important this never gets out, Mike. My friends would never forgive the lies.'

He looked across the fields, then back into my eyes, and thanked me for the silence. From me and the lads. He knew at least four of us had been involved, and that worried him. A secret shared is a secret lost. But time had proven that we could be trusted. Not so much as a murmur of suspicion had been whispered. No drunken boasts down the pub or hints dropped: the secret was safe.

It bothered me that the same people who'd put pressure on him to resolve the situation had then taken the moral high ground once the Travellers had left.

'I guess you're damned if you do, and damned if you don't,' I commented.

'And there are other Travellers,' he added.

'Others?'

'A new camp to be moved on.'

The farmer told me his old university friend had a serious problem on his smallholding. A group of Travellers had been camped on his land for nearly three months. Because of an unclear boundary on one field he was unable to evict them through legal means, and they'd appealed, claiming it was common land and they had historical rights to be there. I promised we'd help, along the same lines, but he'd be the only line of communication. I trusted him but had no idea about his friend.

Within a couple of days he drove back to the Chateau for a more detailed discussion, a wry smile on his face as I opened my front door to join him outside. Again, there was a chill in the air, and as I put on my fleece jacket I noticed he was wearing his typical farmer's jumper, a rust-coloured V-neck. Ironically a style synonymous with both farmers and Travellers.

'Hello, hello,' he said, twice as always.

We shook hands and wandered into the lane, seeking privacy for our delicate conversation.

By the end of our stroll the deal was done. The guys and I would be riding out again.

The smallholding was nearly an hour away on the edge of the fens. I knew the local town names but not the area, and the farmer and I sat in my room and pored over images on Google Earth as he related tales of reported thefts and carnage caused by this Traveller group. In addition to the satellite preparation, I felt safe enough doing a couple of daytime drive-bys, with no fear of recognition so far from my home.

We'd agreed that if I wanted to gather the boys together I'd send an invite by text to meet at a pub to watch a fictitious rugby game. It was to be our Gypsy code, our secret way of confirming the real purpose of the night ahead. Only they'd know it was actually about riding out on another mission. It also meant that if our communications were ever checked all it would show was that I'd made an easy enough mistake about a rugby match.

Again, I'd chosen the Hunters Arms for the meeting as we were all familiar faces in there. Everyone arrived on time, and we sat at our 'War Room' table in the corner, away from the handful of other customers.

I got straight to the point. 'Are you boys all up for a rerun?' I kept my face neutral. I felt it was important that they all made a free choice, with no pressure from me.

'Too bloody right,' answered Tommy, that familiar grin spreading across his face.

'I'm in,' added Will.

'Count me in, too,' confirmed Jason.

So, we were all set. I was relieved to keep the same team. Being involved in the first attack had given us all the experience we needed, and a good reason to keep our pact.

'Just to confirm, guys, you all know exactly what we're signing up for again?'

I looked each of them in the eye, noting their steady confidence, the enthusiasm. I grinned. There was nothing better than being part of something with trusted friends, and we were all buzzing for another adventure. I indicated that we shouldn't discuss it any more in the pub, so we drank up and headed over to my house in Botesdale where I turned on my laptop and opened Google Earth.

As before, I showed them the roads, the approach, the exit routes, the rendezvous point, then went through the timings. The main difference here was that there were no hedges: we'd have to leave the engines running and rely on foot speed to get away. There was a small building, a telephone exchange, near enough to hide the bikes while Tommy and I approached the final yards to the camp.

After this virtual practice mission with the boys, Tommy and I made plans to meet up in Norwich to trawl the charity shops for our disposable outfits. I'd carefully burnt mine from the first trip, and Tommy had promised me he'd done the same with his. Days later we were acting the fool in various shops around Norwich, Tommy's charm working its usual magic on the various members of staff. One thing we struggled to find as a disposable item were the jackets. Riding on a motorbike at that speed really deserved a decent leather, as one fall could shred skin to the bone through a thin fleece. But that kind of gear doesn't come cheap, and we both compromised with army surplus kit, thinking the camouflage pattern added something to our outfits.

Within the week it was time to ride out. Thankfully, there was a light fog near the camp on the night, and we pulled up at the meeting place, again travelling separately to minimize any risk of being identified or caught.

It was only half a mile to the small brick telephone exchange, and it felt like only seconds passed before we were there. My knees had seized up from the hour-long ride so I rubbed them and did some stretches to prepare. Tommy followed suit, and I couldn't see his face to work out if he was serious or taking the piss. Knowing Tommy it was probably the latter, and I was glad of his ability to lighten the atmosphere.

The camp was invisible beyond the shroud of mist, and the fog muffled all sound. It was nearly silent.

I got out the petrol bombs, gave one to Tommy, and nodded. We crept a hundred yards along a water-filled ditch opposite the caravans. In the distance, we heard the familiar high-pitched yip of a dog fox claiming his patch. The ditch was a real hazard for us in the dark. I had no idea how deep the water was, and taking a midnight swim wasn't in my plan.

Tommy paused, and I did, too. He held up his hand in caution. A man was walking away from one of the caravans. We were standing on the road, twenty yards from the field entrance, with not so much as a tuft of grass to hide behind. If he turned our way he'd see us. My heart was thumping. This was crazy. The temptation to run was overwhelming. The man stopped and, in the silence, I heard his zipper before he started to piss. I could even hear the splash, and time seemed to move in slow motion.

I looked at Tommy. He was grinning. I shook my head in disbelief and crouched down in a pointless attempt to hide. Tommy copied me and we stayed there, two dark shapes crouched in the mist while the other man pissed like a horse. Finally he finished, zipped up his flies, and paused. My heart stopped beating, my breath caught in my throat. What the hell were we doing there? He looked up at the night sky, mostly obscured by the low mist, then stretched and continued walking to his caravan. The door clicked shut and a light went on inside.

I leant close to Tommy. 'What shall we do?' I whispered, prepared for a retreat.

The sight of the man had unnerved me, but Tommy said nothing. He simply stood up and walked forward, towards the camp. I followed him to the field entrance. He had his lighter ready, and I held my bottle out next to his for them to be lit together.

The flame took the rags, and we threw. Both bottles exploded against the trailer.

And we ran.

No delay in getting my legs moving this time, but again I felt as if I was running through syrup. I knew I could go faster but my legs felt like jelly. And the noise from the camp was terrifying. The loud bangs of the impact, glass shattering, and then the soft whoosh of the flames. Dogs suddenly barking, men shouting.

As soon as the flames lit the sky Jason and Will had started the bikes, revving the engines ready for the escape. I leapt on the back and we were screaming up the road, side by side. I was holding on with shaking arms, trying to ignore the TT-style riding with pegs grinding on the road round corners. We had separate routes again, splitting apart after half a mile to regroup five miles on. There was no pursuit, no chance of one as we were away so fast.

We met at a pub on a staggered crossroads, pulling in at exactly the same moment. We jumped off the bikes and high-fived, with confident laughter. The euphoria was almost tangible. We were bonded by our actions and enjoying our success. We even stopped at a few pubs on the way back to celebrate. The heady lack of caution was a real contrast to the first outing.

7

Time seemed to pass so quickly. Days, weeks, months. I was keeping my contact with Will, Tommy and Jason to a minimum. We'd talked it through and felt the police would have to start sniffing around soon. Two attacks made it a pattern, and even without official complaints from the victims, we needed to be careful.

My business was going from strength to strength. I'd invested in a small workshop, and a Portakabin for an office, all based in an old pig farm near Dickleburgh, a village near Ledburgh. The owner had long ago stopped keeping pigs and was happy to rent out the vacant buildings. I now had three members of staff – Rick, Dan and Kate. Dan was an old friend, a rugby prop I'd met at Norwich. He was solid in every way, physically and mentally. His skill was welding. Any metals that could be forged together, he was on it, equally happy on a bench or lying under some conveyors. Kate was there to run the office, and free up my diary to go selling. With my new-found responsibilities as a business owner, I felt it was time to move out of the chateau. Although I'd had a great laugh renting with a fun bunch of lads, I couldn't live like a carefree bachelor for ever. Not that my next home was full of angels.

I rented a room in a house in Ledburgh, on Fair Green. My housemate was Terry, another hard-drinking prop forward. My first introduction to him years before was as he exited a local pub head first through a window. It was like a crazy brawl scene from a Wild West saloon, with Terry as the indestructible cowboy. He'd stood up, brushed off the glass, excused himself and gone back inside for the next round.

Rick was going through a tough time at home and had agreed to a trial separation from his wife. There was a spare bedroom in the house, and as Terry and Rick got along well, I floated the idea of him staying with us for a short while. It worked pretty well as we were all old enough to respect personal space and privacy, and most nights we were out boozing. The house was just a wander away from the best pub in town, the Hunters Arms. We spent many evenings walking there and crawling back. Between our house and the pub, Fair Green was a meadow of common land mentioned in the Domesday Book. Years before, the council had dug a small ditch around the green to stop Travellers pulling on vans and caravans. The ditch had been named Wigbys Way by some wags from the pub – my housemate had been known to crawl the length of it to get home. One night when Terry was stumbling back he had tripped over a sleeping horse. Local Gypsies some-times tethered their horses there for grazing, and the startled animal reared up. Terry thought the devil himself had risen from the ground to drag him to Hell. He'd run back into the pub, shaking, and demanded a large whisky.

One Saturday morning, after a particularly heavy Friday session, I was in the kitchen at the back of the house when I heard someone come into the front room. I assumed it was Terry or Rick and went through to say hello.

It was neither of them.

Two of the Smiths stood there. Right there, in my fucking living room. Now, I'm not the tallest guy, but I was head and shoulders over those two. Stupid faces under greasy black hair, dressed in their standard uniform of hoodies, tracksuit bottoms and dirty trainers. The front door had been left wide open, as it often was, and they'd decided to chance their luck. The expression on their faces as I walked in was a picture.

'What the fuck?' I blurted out.

They took one look at me and ran. A second after I got over the initial shock I chased after them, barefoot. Two quick corners and they split, realizing I was on my own. I rounded a third corner and there was a Smith, side on to me, breathing hard. I hit him with a running punch, knocking him over a low wall into a front garden.

'Fuck off, fuck off!' he tried to shout, as I twisted and rolled on top. I knew the little bastards were known to carry knives so I had no sympathy, dropping a forearm across his nose, and aiming my elbow at his eye as he turned away. Two more strikes to his face took the fight out of him, and I climbed off. If I hadn't been barefoot I would probably have started a calculated series of kicks to any soft bits I could reach, but I settled for words, offering dire threats as to what I'd do if I saw him again.

'And now fuck off.'

I left him bleeding on the front lawn, and walked away. I'd hurt my hand with the first punch, and cut my foot running along the street. Still, I'd earned a drink and I headed back via the Hunters Arms, hoping it would be open. I peered through the lead-glass windows and Tracy the barmaid came to the door, as always with that lovely smile on her face.

'What you up to, Mike?'

'Could do with an early pint, Tracy.'

She opened the door. 'Thought you'd had enough last night.' She laughed, then saw my bare feet. 'Where's your shoes, you daft sod? You've cut your foot. Don't go bleeding on my clean floor.'

Tracy poured me a well-earned beer, and for the first of countless times, I told the tale of yet another Smith-chasing adventure. I was in there until closing. Terry had got back to find the door wide open and nobody at home, and had headed over to find me at the pub downing pints. He laughed and agreed the Smiths had been lucky – God knew what would've happened to them if all three of us had been there. It was a memorable night. I was enjoying the banter and my growing folk-hero status, a man happy to take on the villains.

And it seemed that few folk in Ledburgh were prepared to fight back. Even those paid a wage to keep the peace. Morrisons had just built a supermarket in town, and I was told how the Smiths would simply walk in, fill a trolley with shopping and walk out, challenging anyone to stop them. This had gone on for a few weeks before it was referred to area level and Morrisons commissioned extra security. The Smiths responded by filling three trolleys, and while one was being held and argued over, the other two were loaded into a van, the third abandoned in the doorway with a litany of abuse.

It seemed they felt untouchable, above the law. And that had to change.

8

Saracen UK was going from strength to strength. I had more than a dozen full-time employees, and a dozen sub-contractors. We were a regular fixture at most chicken-processing factories. There was a high profit margin in stainless steel, and I'd focused on the chicken industry for purely financial reasons: the one meat that all religions ate in abundance was chicken.

The meat-processing industry was awash with cash, constant projects taking place in sites all over the UK and Ireland. The large companies hadn't realized they were being ripped off by their own group engineers, under pressure to justify their little empire, salaries and offices, so the constant changes in their factories were being driven just as hard from inside as out. If they'd got it right the first time they wouldn't have to keep changing it, would they? But, for us, it was money for old rope. These were golden times, not that I wasn't putting in the hours to make the cash.

My normal working week was eight days long. Seven days a week plus one or two night shifts. I could be staying near Hull fitting refrigeration plant into a new build, leaving the site at five and driving to Suffolk to move machinery overnight while they were cleaning down. Then, at two in the morning, I'd head back to Hull for a few hours' kip and be back on duty: I'd landed a cushy number doing night cover at a herb factory. They ran twenty-four/seven in harvest mode and needed an engineer on constant call. I fitted a single bed in my van, and if they had a breakdown they'd bang on the side and wake me up. Most nights passed without incident so I was earning thirty pounds an hour for being asleep. But I also made sure nobody worked harder than me, wanting to set a good example to the rest of the team.

Especially on jobs like replacing a scald tank in a chicken-processing plant. Over the years the insulation had been replaced with congealed blood and unidentifiable parts of thousands of chickens. It stank. I sent the boys off for a break and did the dirty work myself. I set about cutting up the two-tonne blood clot with a steam lance. By the time they got back, the old tank was clean and ready to take out. I, on the other hand, was not. I was covered in the stuff, head to toe. I went home to get cleaned up and left them to fit the new tank. I'd never ask any of the lads to do something I wouldn't do myself.

As with all engineering firms, we produced scrap steel. Ours was mostly stainless so it held a higher value, and at this time scrap metal was still mostly a cash business with very little traceability – hence it being a target for thieves such as the Smiths: it could easily be sold on to a third party with no questions asked. I used to keep all my scrap money to take my staff and regular contractors away for a few days as a reward. Over the years we'd been on trips to Prague and Krakow. Everything was paid for with the kitty from the moment they all left home until the drop-off. It was all cash money so the tax man never knew. HMRC would've classed a trip like that as a benefit in kind, and the boys would have been taxed on the value. Things like that used to piss me off so much. We worked hard for our money, and surely a little cream here and there was well deserved.

The only non-staff member who came on those trips was Sam, my best customer. He'd helped us out with some technical advice on other jobs, as well as keeping us busy at his own factory. It seemed right to take him along, and it helped that we were firm friends. The trips were like week-long stag dos or rugby tours. In Prague we drank a cellar bar out of Jack Daniel's, and ended up in a strip club that was home to a famous dwarf lap dancer. She came on and did her stuff, and I was drunk enough to be confused as to whether she was really that small or I was just sitting too far away.

The days were filled with going to gun ranges, paint-balling, or visiting places like the salt mine near Krakow. But it was in the evenings that we really let go, celebrating the success of our business with some wild nights out. We worked hard, drank hard and played hard. I was trying to create a rugby-team camaraderie, and was blessed with a great bunch of lads.

Rick was working in a plant being shut down near Uxbridge when he'd been approached by a Scottish engineer, Allan, based in Thailand. Allan had flown over there to remove some plant to be reinstalled in his factory and, expecting all the kit to be ready for despatch, he was woefully ill-equipped to get the machinery ready to load into the containers booked for later in the week. He asked for help. That was the start of a firm friendship that took us all to Thailand for many visits. Rick and I knew we needed extra help to run all the different projects going on. My background was in design and manufacturing and Rick had cut his teeth on the tools in various factories and knew far more than most engineers about keeping a factory going.

We needed another colleague capable of running projects, and I was in no doubt about the man I wanted. Sam had been laughing about our recent trip to Krakow during my last visit to his site. He was working as an engineering manager for a local chicken-processing site, my best customer. Hardly a week went by without us visiting him for anything from pipework to shift covers. We were a one-stop shop for Sam, and had never let him down. I went to see him and sound him out. I'd just been asked to perform a survey on a closed chicken-processing site in Malta. A customer of mine had an option to buy the factory and wanted me to inspect it to see how much kit could be reused. Sam would be perfect for the trip, and it would give me some quality time to get to know him and hopefully lure him to Saracen. I asked if he could get a few days off to come to Malta, and he readily agreed.

We had four days booked on the island. After a couple of phone calls a chap turned up with the keys to show us round the factory. To our surprise and pleasure we were finished within thirty minutes. Every part of the factory was mild steel, either rusty or painted, and new EU regulations meant that it had to be stainless or galvanized. There was nothing reusable in the whole building. Our client would be buying a shell with a licence, and the investment would be massive. Sam and I couldn't stop laughing as we headed to the nearest pub: a four-day job was over in less than an hour. We now had three days of living it up in Malta on expenses. However, Sam always had an eye for the ladies, and I was quickly abandoned as he worked his charms, although he did at least wave at me as he left the bar with the girl on his arm.

I headed back to the digs alone. The next morning I called his phone a few times with no answer. That annoyed me as the whole idea of taking him out there was to discuss the chances of getting him to work for Saracen. Now I was Billy No-Mates while he followed his dick around. I decided not to waste any more time there, and as I had the car, I headed over to Gozo, a small island north of Malta. On the ferry I met a chicken-factory engineer Sam and I knew. He was on holiday. It was a mad coincidence, and we sat chatting on the crossing. I told him why I was travelling alone and he laughed. I forced a smile, but it had certainly taken the shine off the trip for me.

The next time I saw Sam was at the airport. My recruitment plan had been scuppered.

A few days later we had a chance to chat, and I promised him enough work if he went self-employed. Now I had a team that could literally take on the engineering world, and when Rick's relationship with Allan, the Scottish engineer in Thailand, secured some installation work over there, we were more than ready for the task ahead. With no financial risk to us – the deposit covered the cost of the trip – the lads and I boarded a plane to the Land of Smiles.

The kit we were going to install had been standing in the factory yard in Thailand for almost a year. This would be the first automated line in the country so it was a big deal in the chicken industry. Three weeks of installation and commissioning, one week staying around in case anything went wrong.

The heat was oppressive – the air seemed heavier than it was back home – and stepping out of the shade was asking for sunburn. But the country was stunning. On the drive out to the factory we left Bangkok behind and headed into rural Thailand. Lush forests lined roads edged with sheds and shacks, people's actual homes. The level of poverty for the masses was humbling. I couldn't understand the constant smiles on people's faces, as they seemed genuinely happy in their basic lives.

The project went like a dream. My steel-work background, Rick's flair for bodging things together, Dan's welding prowess and Sam's technical knowledge ticked every box. Ahead of schedule we designed, installed and commissioned a full evisceration line. Allan was so pleased he offered to take us to the coast at Pattaya for the remainder of our time in the country.

With him as a guide we had the craziest week of our lives. Drink was cheap, bars were everywhere and full of attentive women eager to befriend any foreign visitors. By now I'd got acclimatized to the weather and was enjoying eating and drinking all day, then wandering around the markets in the evenings. This was the first of many trips to Thailand spread over a three-year period and they all followed the same pattern. We'd get the work done and head down to Pattaya for some recreation.

Those projects were a fantastic experience. Yes, the work was hard, incredibly hot, and the pressure to deliver was very real, but the money was rolling in, and I was often away from Ledburgh, far from the threat of the Smiths or any other Traveller looking for revenge.

9

Business at home and abroad was going well, booming in fact, Sam had settled in a treat and we were making some serious money. But the non-stop work, along with the nagging worry of either being tracked down by an angry Gypsy from one of the burnings, or ending up on the sharp end of a Smith knife, was exhausting. The Thailand experience had combined hard graft and a holiday, but I realized I needed a different kind of break, a proper trip away from it all, on my own.

To some people going away on holiday alone might seem a little strange, but I've had a fiercely independent streak from an early age. Before family days out walking in the hills, I'd pore over Ordnance Survey maps with my parents, discussing the route in advance because they knew I'd always hare off ahead, disappearing over some distant horizon on my own. By the age of eleven I was happy to cycle from north Norfolk down to Aldeburgh on the Suffolk coast to visit my grandparents. It was an arduous trek involving map-reading and trying to avoid getting squashed by dozens of articulated lorries thundering by within inches of my wobbling wheels. I look back in wonder when I compare my boyhood to that of eleven-year-olds these days, most of whom can hardly ride a bike, let alone navigate bypasses and A-roads without a smartphone.

It was early one Saturday morning as a seventeen-year-old that I first thought of venturing further from home. My mother had asked me to collect some bread from Edwards, the local baker, so off into town I headed ... with zero intention of coming back clutching a fresh loaf. No, I had more ambitious plans that day than simply doing some errands.

I'd just been issued a one-year passport, a slip of pink card with my photograph glued on, and the outer curve of the post-office stamp covering my left ear and eye. My newest and most valued possession. I also had my building society book, and the combination of the two items, with the rucksack on my back, offered freedom. By lunchtime I was at the desk in Norwich airport, my savings account empty, but my pocket full of cash.

I called my parents at eleven that evening to let them know I was safe and sound, and where I was. Mum answered the phone, asking after her bread. I promised I'd bring her a baguette home from Toulouse in southern France.

Once my parents knew I was okay, or at least that I was bloody-minded enough to ignore any pleas to get on the next flight home, I headed for the coast and slept on the beach in a small town called Gruissan, making a hobo-style shelter under the veranda of an unoccupied house. It became a lengthy summer of all-night discos followed by sleeping until lunchtime and making new friends from every country around Europe. I loved it. The sense of adventure in me was irrepressible, and the next year I hiked through France and Belgium to spend some time in Luxembourg, including an escapade that would make the newspapers back in Britain.

Towards the end of my trip I'd indulged in a cabin with a shower to clean up as I'd spent a few nights camped out in the surrounding forest. It was a peaceful and serene hideaway, yet after a blissful scrub down I suddenly heard a gunshot. I pulled on some clothes and ran outside to see an elderly man pointing at the lake and shouting for help. I sprinted over to the handrail to see a body floating in the water, face down, a halo of blood around its head. I pulled off my shirt, kicked off my trainers and dived in, surfacing beside the man. I actually thought he was already dead until I turned him over in the water and he spoke a few words. Remembering my swimming lessons, I got his head on my chest and back-paddled to the bank. With helping hands from various onlookers, we dragged him out of the water and laid him on his back on the path. A few more folk had gathered by now, watching the drama unfold. Some just stood there shell-shocked, staring. He had a serious wound on his forehead, and had stopped breathing, so I started CPR.

After I seemed to have spent an age pumping his chest and blowing air into his lungs, an ambulance pulled up and the paramedics took over, placing an oxygen mask over the man's face. I sat back to gasp for clean air only to see a policeman, gun drawn, bark a curt instruction at me. I had no idea what he was saying, and I was simply taken away, still soaking wet, to sit in the back of his car. I was locked in. Adrenalin and nerves kicked in and I clearly remember shaking and feeling scared. What on earth had I done wrong by diving into a lake and trying to save some poor bloke's life?

Finally another officer arrived, thankfully fluent in English, and the situation changed dramatically as I explained what had happened. I was swiftly taken from the car, and my hand was shaken by all the police and others gathered around while my back was patted through the grey blanket some kind soul had thrown around my shoulders. It turned out I'd been a suspect of sorts when the police arrived because the guy in the lake had murdered his wife, the local and beloved mayoress of the town. He'd then walked down to the park, climbed over the railings and shot himself in the head. That was the bang I'd heard, which explained the blood in the water and the missing part of his forehead. He'd probably told me to piss off as I turned him over in the water, but he'd spoken in German so I hadn't understood him. Despite all of our efforts, he died four days later.

A few days later the story was wired back to the local paper in Norfolk, accompanied by a big picture of my grinning mug, which was how my parents knew where that summer had taken me on my travels.

Years later, with the spirit of adventure still calling, I planned a trip halfway across the world, even though I now had a growing business and responsibilities to my burgeoning team of staff. I've always loved visiting the US, and a road trip to California had been beckoning for a few years. Within a week I had flights and car hire booked, and was looking forward to a three-week road trip along the Pacific coast. Saracen was flat out on various sites, and everything was under control, or so I presumed.

Thinking back on that trip now, and realizing that I always seemed to attract trouble on my travels, or at home, what eventually happened was perhaps no surprise.

A sign of my knackered state: I slept for the whole twelve-hour flight, and had to be gently shaken awake on the runway in Los Angeles. A quick bus ride later and I arrived at Avis car hire. I'd decided to treat myself and hire a convertible Mustang, which I'd reserved from the UK the week before.

'Good morning, Mr Woodhouse.' I was greeted by a walking toothpaste advert in an immaculate white shirt emblazoned with the Avis logo. 'How was your flight?'

'Lovely, thank you. I've already reserved a car. Is it ready?'

'Valeted and good to go.' He walked around the desk and showed me to the forecourt. 'But I have something for you to look at first as an option.' He beamed at me. 'An upgrade of sorts.'

He picked up two sets of keys and I followed him outside into the heat of the Californian sun. First he started up a beautiful dark blue Mustang, the engine roaring under his foot, heavy on the pedal. Then we rounded the corner to see a real beast of a car, a race-tuned Shelby Mustang. Dark metallic green with two gold stripes. It looked as good as it sounded, the pistons thundering across the lot when he fired it up. 'Wow.'

I knew I'd been played by the salesman, but I happily paid the extra three hundred dollars and purred out of the car park. The dashboard had a built-in satnav, and I keyed in the details of the hotel I'd booked in Los Angeles for the first two nights. As I went to pull into the hotel car park a small white convertible nipped in front of me. A pretty girl flashed a dazzling smile of apology, and was instantly forgiven. I followed her car up three levels and swung into the adjacent parking bay. When I pumped the throttle, the supercharged engine seemed to shake the building. It set off about a dozen car alarms and the noise was deafening. By now we were both standing by our vehicles and started laughing. This is crazy, I thought. I've only just got off the plane. This car was out of my league, this girl was out of my league, but it was happening. I gestured the offer of a drink to her, the noise level still prohibiting any actual conversation, and she nodded. I retrieved my bag and locked the car. When I got out she was waiting. Was it me or the car she liked? I didn't care. We headed over to the elevator. As the door closed out the sound of the alarms, we turned to face each other.

'I'm Mike.' I smiled. 'I'm over here from the UK.' I offered my hand.

'I'm Monica.' She laughed, reaching out to take it. 'Nice to meet you, Mike.'

'So are you staying here or just visiting?'

'I'm meeting some friends in the bar,' she replied. 'But just for a quick drink.'

'Well, maybe we could get some dinner afterwards.' I'd decided it was win or bust.

'Yes.' She smiled, showing perfect white teeth. 'That would be nice.'

We arranged to meet in the bar in an hour's time, so I headed for a shower. I tried to check my excitement as I got ready, not really believing that the gorgeous woman I'd met within hours of touching down in the US would actually be waiting for me upstairs. And as I walked into the bar I wasn't expecting her to be there. But there she was, looking fantastic. I was grinning as I sat down beside her and started chatting. Monica told me she was half Brazilian and half Bolivian, and that she was a nurse in Los Angeles. She'd become an American citizen through her work and her qualifications, and by her residence in California. We were getting along really well, and it was obvious there was some serious chemistry going on. Then suddenly she went quiet, and I thought I'd asked too many questions.

'Mike,' she said, her face abruptly serious. 'There's something you should know.' Her voice cracked as she spoke.

'What's wrong, Monica?'

'I'm married,' she whispered. 'I married an Iranian

man to get him his green card so he could stay here. I'd never even met him until the day we got married. He's a bad man involved in drugs.'

I could see that she found it difficult to talk about him so I changed the subject. We chatted about the UK and my life there. After a while the mood lightened and she was smiling again. We arranged to meet the next day so she could show me round LA.

We spent the next three days enjoying the sights of LA, and I couldn't have wished for a better guide. Monica spoke Portuguese, Spanish and perfect English. On the fourth day she arrived with a red mark on her face and in tears.

'I'm worried, Mike,' she said. 'My husband knows about you. Somebody saw us together in the car. He swore he's going to hurt you, and there are people looking for the car.'

Getting angry and jealous in a fake marriage seemed crazy to me, but Monica was special and I guessed his original feelings had changed.

'We should leave town,' Monica pleaded. 'Head north, up to San Francisco.'

I fly halfway across the world for some peace and quiet, and suddenly I'm part of a getaway. Monica was desperate to leave town and, of course, I wanted to help this lovely woman. We drove out of LA and headed up the Pacific coast, a dream journey that turned into two weeks of driving heaven through Yosemite Park, over into Nevada, right down to San Diego where I was dropping off

Monica before I headed into Mexico. It had been an intense time together, a chance for both of us to forget the troubles of our daily life. Monica had had a chance to be herself without the presence of a volatile partner, and I had had the space to forget the small-town strife, the battles with the Travellers and the stresses of growing a business. We both knew that we were sharing something that was no more than a passionate holiday romance.

We said our goodbyes on the beach front, both sad, yet invigorated by the special time together we'd experienced.

'Will you be okay?' I asked, concerned for her safety. The stories she'd told me about her fake husband were worrying, and violence was his way of life.

'I'll be fine,' she said. 'He needs me, so I'll be safe.'

Monica had friends in San Diego, a place to go for a while to work things out. We kissed farewell, and I drove off to Mexico. I was hoping to go scuba-diving before flying home. Home to confront yet more violence? It seemed to dog my existence, even when I was on holiday.

A day later I was in a boat with half a dozen American students, sailing away from the Mexican coast towards some famous reef dives. I started to do a preliminary check on the gear, valves and seals, basic safety procedure.

'This gear is ancient,' I exclaimed to the crew, pointing out some perished and cracked seals. After a lengthy and heated debate with the dive leader we turned back. I was disappointed, but you don't take chances twenty metres underwater. It ended my trip on a damp note, even though I hadn't actually got into the water, but I felt relaxed enough, recharged even, to get back to Saracen and home, and to deal with any problems that might have arisen in my absence.

10

After returning from my tumultuous holiday in the US, I was splitting my social time between the Hunters Arms, and a new wine bar, which had opened in the town centre. I liked the crowd that used the new bar, and most of the customers frequented both venues. It was a pretty eclectic mix of folk from farming and white-collar backgrounds. The two things that seemed to typify the customers, a disposable income and a cheerful outlook on life, meant there was always a lively buzz in both bars. The Hunters Arms focused more on draught beer, and the slightly more sophisticated wine bar pushed spirits, bottled beer and decent wine. I enjoyed drinking in both, forming good friendships as I settled more and more into the wider community of the town. With the amount of money I was putting into the till at the wine bar, I pulled out my chequebook when an opportunity came up to buy it.

The couple who had opened it were going through rough times, and their business was suffering. I agreed to settle a list of debts in return for the keys, and within a few weeks I was the proud owner of the wine bar.

At first it felt strange to be a publican again. My last experience of running a pub in Norwich had ended badly, although quitting had hardly been my choice. You could even say I had unfinished business as a landlord.

The problem, and the joy, of running a pub is being the face behind the bar. If you're not strong enough as a character it can be an impossible job. A public house is just that. Anyone can come in. The good and the bad.

Now, I'd always had a personal crusade against drugs, chemical drugs, or dirty drugs, as I called them. Happily, weed fell outside this moral stance. As the bar and club I'd managed back in Norwich were so busy, dealers saw them as prime retail space. I disagreed. That developed into a series of ever more angry and physical confrontations. I was paying my doormen to keep the dealers out, and the dealers were paying the doormen to let them in.

One busy Saturday night I made eye contact with a scrubby little weasel I knew was pushing drugs. We had a history, and he'd been barred months before. He clocked me heading his way and bolted out of the front door. I turned and ran through the beer garden to vault over the back wall, forgetting the drop was at least eight feet on to the road below.

I landed heavily, later finding out that I'd broken my heel. But I also landed within arms' reach of the dealer who thought he'd escaped. I swung him against the wall with a dull thud. We wrestled, and I twisted him under me as we hit the deck. Two quick punches to the side of his head and he curled up in a foetal position, defeated. I scrambled off him and started kicking.

'Don't . . . fucking . . . come . . . back.'

Each word was punctuated with a boot to his torso. A few customers had come outside to see what the commotion was about, so I left him on the pavement and went back inside. My doorman wouldn't meet my eye. We both knew the score, and it was uncomfortable. But now wasn't the time for that conversation. I was limping, serious pain in my right foot. Adrenalin had masked the injury during the fight, but now I knew something was seriously wrong. I could hardly put any weight on it at all. It was a few days later that I was hobbling down London Street into the city centre when a skinny guy, early twenties, lank hair and tattoos over his neck, approached me.

'Are you Mike? The landlord from Tusk?'

I nodded, instantly on guard. 'Can I help you with anything?' I replied, while thinking that pushing him under the nearest bus would do the world a favour.

'If you don't back off and let us in, we'll kill your dog.' A strong Geordie accent delivered the threat.

'You'll do what?' I asked, stunned.

'Kill your fucking dog. You've been told now, so back off.'

I was too shocked to react. I should've decked him there and then, but I just stood and watched him slink away, like waste down a drain.

I hobbled back to the pub as fast as I could. Benson, my German pointer, welcomed me through the door. Okay, he was safe for now. I rang the police and relayed the conversation I'd just had with the drug dealer's friend.

'I'm sorry, Mike,' sympathized the officer, 'but there's

very little we can do in the real world. You won't be the first or the last.'

He went on to detail how those guys would come into the pub, make a fuss of the dog, cut its throat with a box-cutter, then simply walk out, leaving the dog to bleed out on the floor.

I put the phone down. Ten hours later I'd moved out of the pub. As much as it sat in my gut for months to think those bastards had won, I couldn't have risked Benson coming to harm. From there I'd relocated to Ledburgh and got a job as a welder, then become an engineer, and ultimately the owner of my own company. And life was good. You could ask why I'd returned to running pubs when things were going along so well, but I firmly believed things would be different in a small market town.

The wine bar was already established, so all I had to do was maintain the business as it was. One of the main things that appealed to me about the property was the flat that came with it. Three rooms, previously used by various companies as offices, had real potential. I haggled a three-month rent-free period in return for a basic con-version. Now I had a nice gaff above my own bar. The only problem was the lack of parking. I went to my friends who owned the Saracen's Head just down the road. For an annual fee I secured a space, but once I started park-ing there I soon found that the wall around the car park was a favourite hangout for the Smiths and their gang.

What was it that attracted kids from normal families to hang around and idolize that scum? Adopting the uniform of hoody, tracksuit bottoms and cheap black trainers, they loped around chain-smoking, swearing, spitting and pushing each other in front of old folk trying to get by on the pavement. Generally being a pain in the arse.

Back in North Walsham, where I'd grown up, there was the town clock, a famous feature of the Norfolk market town, where adolescents would gather, just sitting around. My father had always said that if he drove by and caught my brothers or me sitting there he'd pull over and take a belt to us. That lesson must have taken root in me and explained my reaction to the gang of youths sitting on the wall.

There were always two or three of the teenage Smith family there, and perhaps half a dozen or more tagalongs. It always surprised me that a couple looked much older: guys in their mid-twenties, thin attempts at moustaches, skin blemished through poor diet and poorer hygiene, laughing at every comment from their pathetic heroes, and encouraging each other to upset the next passer-by.

As I parked my van there, they'd bang on the side panels, trying to get a reaction out of me. I always stared them out, refusing to look away and making my contempt clear. But I never forced the issue. I knew there was CCTV, but it would be very easy for them to damage my van during the night. This uneasy game went on for a few weeks, then seemed to ease off once they got bored.

After a particularly hard day on site I backed up my van as usual and was looking forward to a well-earned beer in the bar. Thumping on the side of the van suddenly broke the silence and kicked me into retaliation.

I always had a length of thick electrical flex in the door pocket of the van. I'd seen for myself the serious damage caused by a blow from this stuff. The outer rubber casing makes the first impact before the inner core of twenty-millimetre copper makes a second as the casing compresses. The result is an open wound down the bone. Back in the day, before the yellow badge system had come in and registered bouncers, lots of doormen in Norwich used to keep foot-long pieces up their sleeves. I grabbed my flex and jumped from the van, exhaustion replaced instantly with rage and the desire to teach the bastards a lesson.

Four guys, one Smith plus three tagalongs. Easy odds for an angry man against an over-confident opposition. They'd almost turned away, laughing, not expecting a reaction after weeks of taunting had failed, when I caught the first one across the upper arm. He fell to the ground clutching his shoulder in shock and pain.

'Right, you fuckers, who's next?' I bellowed, as they backed away, keeping the wall between us. When I stepped to the wall they backed off further.

'Fuck off, you nutter,' one shouted, as I scrambled over the wall, flex in hand, almost landing on the lad on the ground. His groaning changed pitch as I deliberately stamped on his hand in my work boots.

Now the chase was on. They could run – I had to admire their speed down the alley and round the corner.

Despite years of rugby I lost ground from the off, blaming my heavy footwear. I returned to find the injured lad still sitting there, holding his shoulder and looking at his bruised hand. I knelt beside him.

'If you little bastards don't leave my van alone I'll hunt you down, one by one, and kick the living shit out of you.'

It was an angry threat born of adrenalin and temper, the built-up frustration of seeing how a few yobs could ruin a community. I moved my van to a safer place, kn-my heart I'd poked a wasps' nest. There was no way it would have lasted the night parked there, and as I walked to the bar I remonstrated to myself: Bloody stupid. Should have ignored it as before. Now look what you've done. I was angry with my violent response. I'd escalated trouble in the town centre. I'd made it personal again.

On many occasions following that night I'd walk through town to fetch something and they'd stand there, emboldened by numbers. They certainly knew who I was and were trying to intimidate me. And it worked to a point. As I walked down from the bar late at night to fetch a kebab or visit another pub, I felt uncomfortable and vulnerable. So I forced myself to stride through them if they stood in a group on the pavement, holding eye contact to offer an unspoken challenge. I was nervous but never let them know. And I wasn't alone in my feelings.

The number of folk visiting the pubs and restaurants in the evenings was dropping on a weekly basis. The sheer numbers of that Traveller clan, and all their hangers-on, were threatening. Quite simply they'd taken control of the town centre.

I was walking through the town early one Saturday morning, still feeling a bit fuzzy from a big party the night before. The wine bar was going really well, we'd been rammed again, and the atmosphere was buzzing.

As I turned the corner into the market place I was confronted by yet another broken window. Two sheets of plywood had been fitted over the front of the pizza and kebab shop. Without asking, I knew what had happened. And, sure enough, the owner was outside, brush in hand, talking with another resident.

'They came back later and smashed the window,' he lamented.

'Little bastards,' the old man muttered, patting the owner on the arm before wandering off.

'Need I ask?' I said mournfully.

'Twenty years my family's been here, Mike.' His voice wobbled, and tears welled in his eyes. 'We love this town. It's breaking my heart.'

I felt for him, I really did.

'Those bloody Smiths,' he spat. 'They came here as I was locking up. Asked for money, and all the food I had left. I told them, "No, go away. Don't you threaten me."'

He was shaking with emotion, still raw from last night. They'd continued to threaten him, stopping just short of actual violence.

'I drove them off, but it was made clear they'd be back.'

Because he'd stood up to their threats, the cowards

had returned in the early hours and smashed his front window.

'And who's going to stop them?' he shouted. 'The police? That useless CCTV camera?'

A single camera covered his part of the high street, the only one in Ledburgh, and it had been out of action for months, the council claiming they didn't have the resources to get it working. His frustration and feeling of abandonment were clear. I sympathized with him, and told him things would get better some day, and walked into town.

Did I believe what I'd said? Not really. I was convinced the town was lost. This was the eleventh business to suffer the same fate at the hands of those feral youths. The high street looked more like Beirut than a pretty Norfolk market town. The cost and the heartache to the business owners was beyond estimate. While the council had welcomed a new Tesco with open arms, the high street was being attacked and undermined from all sides.

Some of the shop-owners had left the wooden boards up for much longer than they'd needed to, and I wondered if that was in protest towards the council and the police. But it had little effect – the officials never visited the town they were meant to represent and protect. All it was doing was dragging the whole neighbourhood down into despair.

The police station was now largely unmanned. If you went to the door you had to use a handset to talk to some distant phone operator who had no local knowledge of the area or the problems the town was facing. You were more likely to see the Queen wandering down the high street than a bobby on the beat.

The town had been actively surrendered to the gang. I heard story after story about how they were demanding money or goods, or how windows would get broken. And they did.

I couldn't help but wonder why my wine bar had remained untouched. They knew me, and they hated me. It would've been an easy target. But they never attacked the bar. Never tried to come in, or even look through the windows. Was it because I'd taken a stand?

Anyway, it was the ideal gathering point for more and more local shop-owners to call in and talk about their problems. Because of my open stance on the Smiths, and my vocal attitude to dealing with them, my opinion was sought. I was proud that folk came to me for support, and with that feeling came responsibility.

Something had to change. And fast.

11

The bar was always busy, and every Friday it was absolutely rammed. Drinkers in Ledburgh flocked to it, and word had got around that we were the 'in' venue. To be honest, I wasn't surprised: to say I had a successful track record in promoting bars was an understatement.

Part of my old job working at the nightclub in Norwich had been running promotions. I had a natural flair for marketing ideas, and as a few of the local newspaper journalists frequented our club it was pretty easy to get media attention. We were always busy on Thursdays, and absolutely packed on Friday and Saturday nights. The only way to up our income was to introduce a new night. I suggested a Wednesday event themed on a different film each week, with fancy dress and drink offers. It was agreed so we set about forming a list of suitable movies. *The Blues Brothers*, *Pulp Fiction*, *Grease* and *Summer Holiday* were all a huge success. We had a large screen showing the film, and if the punters made the effort with fancy dress we gave them free admission.

'We're running low on suitable films,' I told the owners in a planning meeting.

'How about *The X-Files*?' one of the bar staff chipped in. 'There's a dance mix of the theme music in the charts at the moment, and fancy dress could be just about anything.'

It seemed like a sound enough idea. The flyers were ordered and the marketing organized. The promotions consisted mainly of me and another member of staff getting dressed up and posing in photos for the local paper a few days in advance, then handing out flyers in the city centre. I duly made the appropriate calls and we arranged to meet the next day for a photo shoot. I have to say we excelled ourselves on the fancy dress, donning green latex alien heads, faces, hands and weird sunglasses. We dressed in black from head to toe and wielded massive spray-painted water guns.

After scaring various old folk and kids while handing out some flyers, we found ourselves posing for photos in the bushes at the top of the Castle Mall shopping centre. We felt as ridiculous as we looked so it was some relief to finish and head back to the club.

'We've still got a couple of hundred flyers left,' I noticed. 'Let's hand them out here.'

I'd suggested we wait at the top of Prince of Wales Road by the bank, next to a huge pedestrian crossing that was busy from every direction. We stood on the wide pavement enjoying some more banter, and handing out the remaining flyers to potential clubbers. Just before we'd finished we heard a blare of sirens coming from every direction, the increasing volume bouncing off the surrounding buildings.

'Something's going on,' I shouted to my mate. 'And pretty serious by the number of sirens.'

It was at that moment I was felled, like a tree, hit squarely from behind. As I dropped, my colleague passed me, heading for the pavement in similar fashion. Strong arms held me down, and my initial reaction to fight was deterred by the knees in my back. My arms were pinned.

'What the fuck? Who are you?' I was shouting, still trying to wriggle free. Then I saw the uniforms. Lots and lots of police uniforms. We were thrown into the back of a patrol car and driven to Bethel Street station, where officers ripped off our alien masks and frogmarched us inside to stand before a stern sergeant at the booking-in desk. Down the corridor, thankfully, I saw a familiar face, an old rugby friend. 'Graham,' I called to him in desperation. 'Graham, mate.'

He slowly turned and looked at me. 'Mike? Is that you?' He walked up the corridor towards me.

'Of course it's me!' I shouted, forgetting that even without the mask I was still heavily disguised as an alien.

'Oh, you bloody idiot.' Graham was fighting a huge grin off his face. 'You absolute idiot.'

I was in no mood for humour, my arms and ribs still sore from the pavement.

Graham spoke to his colleagues. 'I know this man,' he explained. 'He's no bank robber. A complete nutcase, yes, but definitely not a bank robber.'

The atmosphere quickly changed, and the sergeant explained that our stunt had triggered a heist alert: an off-duty manager from Barclays, the biggest branch in East Anglia, had been driving past the bank and seen two masked men with guns. Calls were made and every armed officer in Norfolk had sped towards the city centre.

We were cautioned and told off for being stupid enough to stand outside a bank in those outfits with fake guns. We could hardly argue. We'd simply forgotten where we were. And on the plus side the arrest certainly helped the marketing. The next day the photos of us crouching in the bushes were syndicated out to the national papers, and the *Daily Sport* ran a full page on the 'Alien Bank Heist Drama'.

The wine bar didn't manage a promotional story in a national newspaper, but we didn't need that kind of coverage, not with the numbers walking through the door. We'd cornered the market for the middle-aged, middle-class folk of the area with money to spend. There was the usual crowd, which we seemed to share with the Hunters Arms on the other side of town, and on that particular evening a few rugby mates as well. A buzzing roomful of smiling faces loosening up for the weekend. This had the look of a good night ahead.

Part of being a good publican is mixing with the clientele, so I was out from behind the bar chatting with customers, while the two girls on the till were coping just fine. My friend Tony came in, always a welcome sight. Everyone knew Tony, who was offered smiles and handshakes as he entered the room. A renowned grafter, Tony was a Traveller who'd settled in Ledburgh and become a firm part of the larger community, respected on both sides of the divide. He was held in high regard by the

Romany and the gorgias, who all looked on him as one of their own, and was famous for working seven days a week, clearing houses and selling antiques and furniture, as well as dabbling in second-hand cars.

Where the Smiths were concerned, Tony walked a strange line. He was a bit like Switzerland, a neutral with no publicly stated opinions of them. I think he saw them as an embarrassment to the Travelling community. I had no confusion in my mind – it wasn't a cultural thing for me. I liked and respected Tony as a straight-up guy and a hard worker, and to me, the Smiths were the lowest of the low. My feelings were based on how folk acted, not their ethnicity or social standing.

Anyway, Tony was the ideal regular, great company and a good spender, and he understood bar etiquette like an art form. We'd met in the Hunters years before and I always enjoyed a laugh with him. However, it wasn't Tony who had caught my eye that Friday evening, but the woman on his arm. She seemed almost like royalty in that little wine bar. Long dark hair, slim, in killer heels. Flashing a perfect white smile. And, my God, those eyes. Dark, full of mystery and promise. A man could die happy staring into them.

I swallowed, then checked myself in the mirror. I'd have to look my absolute best even to speak to her. I pushed through the regulars to get to Tony.

'Evening, Tony.' I beamed. 'Everyone must have known you were coming.' I laughed, managing a glance at the beautiful woman on his arm.

'Well, I try to keep a low profile, but what can you do?' Tony shrugged. Typical banter from an old-school pub regular.

'You've outdone yourself tonight, Tony. Are you going to introduce us?' I turned to his stunning partner.

'This is Rhoda, my daughter.' Tony laughed. 'You behave yourself.'

His daughter. Bloody hell, she was lovely. I bent down to kiss her hand as a mock gent, and she laughed. I held her hand for a moment longer than I should have, the gentlest squeeze upon release. And I saw it in her eyes. The challenge, the tease. Oh, this was dangerous but irresistible. Tony grunted something and went across to the bar. Immediately he was surrounded by mates, and soon forgot his daughter.

We chatted, we laughed, we drank. And we drank. I owned the bloody place so we drank what we wanted and plenty of it. Rhoda was friendly, funny, laughed at my jokes, and touched my arm a lot. I was watching for signs, her playing with her hair or some other body language. I didn't have to bother: the eyes said it all. She held my gaze again and again, and I felt like I was drowning.

At the end of the night Rhoda left on her dad's arm, but not before she'd slipped her number into my pocket. I went to sleep, grinning like a Cheshire cat.

Remarkably, she answered my phone call the next day and accepted my offer to take her out on a date. Then a second and a third. I literally couldn't stop thinking about her. We'd now met a few times since that first night in the wine bar, and she'd always looked immaculate. Perfect make-up, perfect hair, perfect clothes. I was hooked, and she knew it. The talk between us was full of innuendo and hidden promises, as we openly flirted with each other. Was part of our attraction the difference in background? I'd told her about chasing the Smiths in the van, and my ongoing scraps with them. She'd just laughed. Being a pure Romany Gypsy she'd never have to worry about them causing her any problems. Her father was well respected in the Travelling community, and she was protected by his reputation. And I'd never tell her about burning out the caravans. That was a darker secret that no Gypsy would forgive.

Or forget.

It was after another busy night at the wine bar, once we'd finished closing up, that a group of my friends had called the Ledburgh Tandoori to check we were okay to go in for a meal. Although I had a lovely date with me, it wasn't Rhoda. I'd tried to get her to come out with me that night but she'd declined. Which turned out to have been a good decision.

So the eight of us, four couples, headed up to the curry house. It had been in the town for decades, and was a firm favourite. I had an arrangement with them that we could dine late while they closed the venue. We were happy to eat while they placed the chairs up and cleaned down. The three other guys were colleagues from work: Sam, now among the management team at Saracen, Dan and Colin. Dan was one of my first employees,

Colin was the youngest. I'd met him at Ledburgh rugby club. At the time he was a failed carpenter, and our ongoing joke was that he was now a failed engineer. Our Thai customer had shaken his head and stated Colin would never be an engineer as long as his arse faced south, and he was probably right. But he was a nice lad and he tried hard. We all had our dates with us, and were enjoying the meal when we heard someone hammering at the door.

The staff were all squeezed into the entrance, and arguing with someone outside. We ignored the fracas, determined not to let it spoil our evening. But it went on and on, escalating into shouting and a series of loud bangs on the front windows.

'Fuck this for a laugh,' I said, wiping my mouth and placing the napkin on the table. 'I'm going to tell them to piss off.' I got up and headed to the door, with Dan and Colin one step behind.

I asked the waiters to move aside and, sure enough, there was the ugly mug of a Smith, mouthing obscenities and threats. I smiled and stepped into the street. There were eleven of them. Shit. Not the best decision I'd ever made, but also not the worst.

'Why don't you run along?' I said, waving them away. 'You're not getting anything here tonight.'

I was trying to hold the lead Smith's stare, but he had a combination of Neanderthal forehead, mono brow, and a wandering eye, which was making it difficult.

I held my ground on the pavement in front of the

97

restaurant. I turned and looked at Dan, who quite simply filled the doorway. Years before, back in our Norwich years, Dan had unwittingly knocked out a head bouncer in a late-night pizza bar. The guy was pushing in and Dan had thrown a single punch, then calmly turned back to place his order. That had started a series of scuffles over the next few months, which had cost me my six best shirts, but Dan had never gone down. After months of trying they just gave up. He was a legend.

One of the Smiths reached over my shoulder and tapped Dan on the chest. 'You're a big fucker. We'll have some fun with you.'

A tiny lift at the corners of Dan's mouth showed his amusement. Then it started. The lad who'd reached over my shoulder was still beside me. I headbutted his face, and we tumbled sideways. Dan moved forwards and landed a peach on the nose of the one directly behind me. He staggered backwards and I looked up to see Dan staring at his own fist as if to say, 'What's wrong with you? Why is he still standing?' Hilarious. His follow-up punch switched the guy out like a light.

Colin and Sam were outside now so there were four of us. Two of the Smiths were still down; a couple were checking on them and trying to help them up. I called, 'Back to back,' as if we'd practised the move, and we set up. I knew the Smiths were natural cowards, masters of the cheap shot from behind, and in this formation they couldn't get near us. Even if they did we met them with a well-aimed punch or a kick. I directed our unit, homing in on three Smiths standing together. Dan dropped another one. 'Back to back,' I called again, and automatically we formed up.

They were absolutely lost, no idea how to deal with us. Half of them had been knocked down, and all had taken a few blows. We were untouched. I was loving it. Colin was proving himself to be a willing scrapper, up at the front and landing some telling punches. Sam was trying to do some kicks but looked more like a hyperactive cast member of *Riverdance*. But we were winning, easily. They'd even resorted to throwing stones, handfuls of gravel from a nearby driveway. Finally one took off his shoe and was trying to hit Colin with his improved longer reach. That was to be our only injury, a light scuff to the forehead from a sock-footed Gypsy swinging his shoe.

Then the sirens. Blue lights. As the police car roared up the hill the Smiths jumped over nearby fences. A couple of them stayed behind, holding up the first lad Dan had punched. They turned and limped away as the police car stopped, and an officer went into the restaurant.

While the car idled outside, lights flashing blue on the brick walls around us, we went back in and sat down. Our food was still warm. Result. We laughed like drains, mostly at Sam's expense. We were all rugby players but he was a footballer: what did you expect?

After a summary of the altercation from the restaurant owner, the police were now engaged in a heated conversation with the staff. The waiters and the owner were complaining bitterly about the constant harassment they were suffering from the gang. The officers stood there in their stab vests and bat belts with a dozen items clipped on. I always wondered how they sat in the car with all that gear. I had to empty a single coin out of my trouser pocket if I was driving more than a mile or it would drive me crazy. They looked like Robocop as they stood there, arms crossed, nodding in sympathy, I presume. One of them approached our table.

'I understand you intervened to protect the staff.'

'Absolutely,' I replied.

Then silence. I'd found over the years that a loose jaw with police officers was a stupid way to go for a whole list of reasons. Be respectful, say the minimum, and don't volunteer information that might extend the conversation.

'Okay, then.' He nodded, glancing around the table. 'Just be careful not to get involved in the future. That's our job.'

We resisted the obvious response, the open goal of a churlish comeback, and watched him waddle out of the curry house in all his protective clobber.

'Don't know about you lot,' I said to my friends, 'but I've worked up an appetite.'

We finished our meal, paid, and headed to the door. The owner took the time to thank us for stepping in, but I could see the worry in his eyes. With good cause. Later that night, long after we'd left, and long after the staff had gone home, all his windows were broken. Every single one. He was the thirteenth victim of that wayward gang.

Considering the ugly street fight I was glad that Rhoda hadn't come along, especially with it involving the Smiths. We'd talked about the van chase, which had initially made her laugh . . . but I'd sensed a slight edge. My general attitude towards the Smiths had caused an atmosphere a few times, and my choice of language included references to them being thieving pikeys, so it was a subject we avoided. And brawling in the road is hardly the most romantic way to spend an evening. I was glad she hadn't witnessed it.

Well, so I thought.

The next day I saw Rhoda in town. She was wearing a scarlet Karen Millen coat. It would've looked wrong on anyone else but was magnificent on her. I walked over to say hello.

'Saw you lot last night.' She was smiling, that dangerous twinkle in her eyes.

'When last night?' I asked, smiling back.

'Outside the Indian. My house is opposite, I watched the whole thing from upstairs.'

Shit, I thought. That's blown it. 'It really wasn't our fault.'

But Rhoda was laughing. 'This way. That way.' She started mimicking a soldier on parade, taking the piss out of my commands during the fight. I felt my cheeks flush, hot with embarrassment. She just smiled and said, 'I thought you were very brave, my hero,' and kissed my cheek. Now I knew she was having a laugh, and it made me laugh, too. Then she turned and walked away on four-inch heels. I watched her until she rounded the corner at the far end of the street, where she glanced back and smiled, knowing full well that I'd still be standing there.

12

Since the van chase and that farce of a court case I'd kept a dialogue going with the police. On the very rare occasion I saw them around I'd always make a point of going and saying hello, trying to draw out some information as to what efforts they were making to halt the local crime wave. I realized the average copper was just as frustrated as anyone else at the lack of resources available to deal with those guys. It made me feel vindicated in my actions. I was taking a direct stand as well as trying to effect change through the proper channels.

After months of fruitless meetings with the local force I was happy to find out that a new chief constable had arrived in Ledburgh and would be based at the largely unmanned station in town. The departing, and probably relieved, incumbent, whose life I'd made hell with constant complaints about the lack of police presence in the area, had told me of this development. All I'd done was point out to him how things actually were.

Worse than ever.

A whole list of businesses had broken windows, and it looked more like a war zone than a quaint market town. And now the population were talking with their feet, staying away from the centre in droves. Even in the daytime it was noticeable how many visitors and shoppers had abandoned the high street.

I booked a face-to-face meeting with the man who'd inherited this mess. And I confess I liked him as soon as I met him.

'I'm Adam,' he greeted me, with a warm handshake. 'Pleasure to meet you.'

You might not think that in ten minutes' time, I thought, taking a seat.

He was intelligent, charismatic, and fiercely ambitious. He sympathized, made all the right noises to soothe my rancour, and calmly explained that there were no resources available to Ledburgh.

'Have you actually walked through the town centre?' I asked, raising my voice a little. 'Have you seen all the boarded-up windows?'

He paused. Manicured fingers propped up his chin, hovering above a brilliant white shirt festooned with the gleaming rank of his office. Not a hair on his head was out of place, and a genuine look of concern momentarily hid his clean white smile. 'I'm aware of the situation in town.'

We were in his office at the rear of Ledburgh police station. Various officers were bustling about, probably trying to look busy for their new boss. It would have been better if they were out on the street rather than inside, shuffling papers and answering the phones. I talked with Adam for a while, and he always had a clever, well-thought-out response to my questions. Watching his underlings buried in admin, I floated the crazy idea that if the police were out on the streets they'd prevent the crime happening in the first place rather than constantly mopping up afterwards. 'Actual prevention has to be more cost-effective than all the paperwork,' I suggested. 'And then making a load of follow-up visits after a crime has taken place.'

'We all agree on that, Mike,' he replied carefully. As always, answering without answering, the consummate professional and adept politician. No doubt destined for great things in the new, procedure-led police force.

We finished the meeting and shook hands. 'See you next week.' It was to be my usual parting shot, indicating that I wouldn't give up, and that there'd be plenty of new crime to justify my coming back. Although I could see he shared a dislike of everything I was angry about, I'd also leave meetings with him convinced he felt I was exaggerating, or that I had my own agenda against the Smith family.

I had to think smart to get the result I wanted.

Through my years of playing rugby I'd made good friends in both the police force and the fire brigade. They'd told me about the percentage of their time dedicated to media relations and media training. As I understood it, the services were as concerned about the public perception of how they were performing as they were about how they actually performed. If you ever saw a fire or police officer being interviewed after an incident, the robotic response sounded like a script prepared by a lawyer, devoid of any opinion or passion. Politics had crept into public service and public perception was paramount.

I came up with a plan.

I started talking to folk in town about a group that had been formed called the Pro Community Forum. It was made up of a large number of concerned local business owners who were angry about the anti-social behaviour, the crime wave Ledburgh was currently suffering, and the lack of policing in the area. The PCF members, I explained, wanted to remain anonymous due to the fear of reprisals, and I was to be their spokesperson. I had lots of friends in the community to recruit, and I risked causing offence to some of my closer friends who wanted more details on the shadowy group I was apparently representing.

The fact that the PCF consisted of just me had to be kept secret. For it to work there had to be an air of mystery about the unknown band of wealthy, concerned business owners.

I picked a date for a public meeting and set about promoting it. I printed posters advertising it, and canvassed shops and business owners to display them. 'It's really important you put the poster up in your front window,' I explained, for the twentieth time that day. 'If we all do it, nobody'll get singled out.'

The Smith gang had put fear on the high street. People were cautious about provoking violence and vandalism with that brazen statement of defiance. Yet to the eternal credit of every single shop and business in town, they all joined in and pinned, tacked and taped up the notice.

From the chippy to the estate agents to the hairdressers and the bookies. Some had even stapled them to the wooden boards where windows were awaiting replacement glass. I felt proud of the townsfolk: there was a real sense of solidarity and a buzz of expectation at what action might come from this public meeting.

I informed the local council, the local paper, and Chief Inspector Adam Hayes that the meeting was taking place. I had confirmations from all except Adam that they'd be attending. He'd gone quiet on me. But I'd expected that. Nobody likes to have their hand forced, and I was certainly pushing the issue. The story ran in the *Ledburgh Express*, a great little local weekly that had started its own campaign against the trouble in town. It was picked up by the BBC and I received a telephone call from Radio Norfolk in Norwich.

'As the nominated spokesman for the PCF, would you be happy to come to the studio and do an interview to inform listeners about the situation in Ledburgh and the public meeting?'

'Yes and yes,' I replied.

With this development I rang Adam. After leaving several messages on his mobile phone I rang his office, and, yet again, was fobbed off with his assistant.

'I'm very sorry, he's not available right now.'

'Can you let him know I'm about to drive to Norwich to be interviewed by the BBC about anti-social behaviour in Ledburgh? I'd like to have some positive quotes from him but seem unable to get in contact.'

There was a pregnant pause on the line. 'You're going up there this morning?'

'On my way out of the door,' I confirmed, thanking her and ending the call. Within three minutes my phone rang. Adam's name appeared on the screen. They say if you answer the phone smiling the other person can hear it – great advice for receptionists. If it's true, Adam certainly heard my grin.

'Hi, Mike, I've been trying to get back to you all week,' he lied outrageously.

But I was too smug to be derailed by any pettiness. 'That's okay, I know you're busy,' I said graciously. 'I'm on my way to be interviewed by the BBC.'

There followed a pointed conversation about salvaging the reputation of the local constabulary pre-interview. I made it clear that the last thing I wanted was to blame the police, and he seemed satisfied.

'So can I confirm to the listeners that you'll attend the meeting?' I asked.

Another pregnant pause. 'Of course. I was always hoping to come,' he replied.

Of course you were, I thought, but was magnanimous enough to let it slide. Thanking him, I got into the car and headed for Norwich.

The interview itself was almost surreal. Along with most folk I'm not fond of hearing my own voice, and wearing headphones, I was getting it in Dolby surround. I tried to get my point across, that if folk in Ledburgh wanted their town back they needed to rock up to the meeting. Pretty sure I'd sounded like a prize dick, I shook the presenter's hand and headed home.

The meeting was a few days later, in the Park Hotel, the biggest indoor space in town that was readily available. It, too, had suffered at the hands of the renegade Travellers, and the management shared a real enthusiasm to host the meeting.

My wine bar was about four hundred yards away, and I left in good time to get there early and greet folk arriving. For days I'd been nervous about whether anyone would bother to turn up, and pictured myself on stage, speaking to an empty room.

As I walked down the hill, I could see what looked like a football crowd surging ahead and behind, all filing into the hotel entrance.

'The phone hasn't stopped all day,' beamed Sally, the hotel owner.

Christ. This was beyond my wildest dreams. I went into the main hall without even pausing to get a drink. The sight that greeted me was incredible. It was rammed. Full to the rafters. The hotel had set out about two hundred seats and they were all full. In fact they were being shared, three folk to every two seats. The raised area around the back looked like a stadium terrace, and it was estimated that at least eight hundred people had squashed themselves into the venue. There was an angry buzz of expectation in the hall, and you could have cut the atmosphere with a knife.

I was gobsmacked. What a result. There was a table at the front and there sat Adam, resplendent in polished buttons and the dark cloth of his uniform. I smiled and walked forward, hand outstretched. He stood and took it, glad to see a friendly face.

In the course of the next hour and a half Adam sat at the front, like a rabbit in the headlights. The hotel had provided a microphone and, by God, the townsfolk made full use of it. Endless stories of theft, break-ins, criminal damage, threats of violence, intimidation. The list went on and on.

'My shed was broken into, all my tools, gone!' A red-faced angry man in his early sixties was shouting into the microphone. 'This is the third time I've lost things out of my own garden. No point even ringing you lot – I end up speaking to someone in bloody Ipswich or even further away.'

He finished his rant to a deafening round of applause from like-minded angry folk, and was followed on to the stage by an elderly lady who told of her garden being trashed. People were queuing to take the microphone and make their point. People terrified of public speaking forgot their fears to have their moment. Mindless vandalism: cars being keyed, garages broken into, petty theft and pointless damage to property.

'You lot are useless.'

'A waste of time.'

There were countless stories of folk attempting to report a crime at what seemed to them an empty police station. I started to feel sorry for Adam. He was still fairly new to Ledburgh, and this situation had evolved over the years before his time. The tirade continued. The language became more colourful as passions increased.

'I can only base our allocation of resources on actual crime figures.' Adam defended his office.

It was time for me to stand up and speak. As the lone face of the Pro Community Forum I was handed the microphone. I waited for a hush, then turned towards Adam. 'The figures that gauge our resources here in terms of police presence are based on reported crime?'

'Correct,' he replied. 'Those figures have fallen year on year in Ledburgh and the surrounding area.'

He'd responded straight from the textbook. Time for some theatrics, I thought. I turned to face the crowd. 'Please raise your hand if you've been a victim of crime in the last year.'

As expected, an ocean of hands went up.

'Okay. Now please keep your hands up if you were a victim of crime and didn't call the police, make a report and get a crime reference number.'

A few hands dropped, but that still left the vast majority in the air.

I turned back to face Adam. He knew what I'd clearly demonstrated, but just to clarify I voiced it for the audience. 'It's not crime that's dropped, it's reported crime that's dropped. And that's because of the breakdown in trust between the community and your office.'

I stated the obvious to a wave of applause. I went on to urge everyone to make sure they got a crime reference number every time they saw or suffered a crime. That would get an official reaction, and presumably we'd be allocated more resources.

More folk, given heart by the show of hands earlier and bonded by their shared experiences of being victims, took the microphone to have their say. And the same family name was mentioned again and again. After Adam had heard yet another horror story from a mother about how her children had been beaten up outside the high school, he held up his hands.

'I'm sorry,' he said. 'I'm sorry for the way we've let you down.'

There was a stunned silence. His honesty had disarmed them. Instead of the expected excuses and blaming everyone else, he'd taken it on the chin.

'It stops tonight,' he stated. 'I give you my word every effort will be made to regain your confidence in your police force.'

It was a hell of a statement to make, and was met with mixed feelings in the crowd. Some people left the hall shaking their heads and muttering that he was all talk. But most nodded at Adam, and many shook his hand. He'd won them over and they wanted him to succeed. We all did.

Within the hour two police vans were parked in Ledburgh town centre, and every night after there was at least one, and police officers patrolling the town became a regular sight.

I later heard that Adam had gone straight round to see Silvanus, the head of the Smith family. Adam had sat down in his living room and calmly explained that things had to change. Silvanus had laughed in his face and asked if he knew how many of the Smiths there were. Adam replied that he knew exactly how many of them there were, but that he had a bigger gang. And a helicopter. He then explained that for every crime committed in Ledburgh he'd pull him in for questioning as a suspect. Silvanus laughed again. He didn't believe him.

Adam left, and a few hours later the police returned to arrest Silvanus. I heard it was for cruelty to horses. That was always going to be an easy charge to level against him: his whole family were infamous for mistreating their animals. The RSPCA were firmly on board and pressing for a prosecution, and had been for years. The problem was proving that the old man owned the horses and not some far-flung, and probably fictitious, relative.

Silvanus was held for the maximum time, and then released. He was rearrested on his way down the station steps. Now he realized he'd met his match, and put word out that any more trouble would answer to him. And it stopped. Just like switching off a tap. Adam had delivered what he had promised, and we had our town back.

For years after that momentous public meeting, and the success that followed it, I was always amused to hear of the different folk claiming to have been involved in the Pro Community Forum. The mystery around it allowed their claims to go unchecked, and as I was the only person involved I was the only one who knew the truth. It was a bluff of epic proportions, yet it had worked.

13

Still high on helping the local community get their town back, I was brought back to earth with a thud.

I couldn't believe what I was hearing. My farmer friend had effectively hired me and the boys out as a service. He'd called me the day before and simply suggested meeting up for a drink. I'd cheerfully agreed: it was so long since the last incident there was no reason for us not to be seen together enjoying a beer.

Well, he had business to discuss.

I arrived at the Hunters Arms early, and was halfway down my pint when he met me at the bar. We'd gone outside to catch the last of the evening sun, setting low across the green, and he told me how another local farmer had just lost a thousand litres of red diesel. A gang of Gypsies were parked on his land, cutting down trees and making a right mess. About a dozen trailers, pulled by a mix of Transit vans and tipper trucks, had set up camp. The farmer had tried asking them to leave and they'd told him in no uncertain terms to get lost. Now the Gypsies were set for a long stay.

Except my farmer friend had promised his friends that the issue would be resolved.

I was furious. 'You've broken every promise,' I snapped.

'Not just to me, but to the other lads. We always said nobody should know or be connected. By offering us out as guns for hire you've confirmed that you're involved. You bloody idiot.' I was shouting, genuinely upset with him.

'I'm sorry, Mike,' he said, crestfallen. 'I thought that after the public meeting you guys would be up for another crack at them. I wasn't thinking straight.'

I was pissed off, and he knew it. But he'd already taken the money. Nothing felt right about it this time, and I told him I'd be in touch. 'If you promise to keep your mouth in check before it ends in tears for all of us.'

A day later I got the lads together. The same text about a bogus rugby match captured their attention, and I carried the beers back to our selected table in the corner of the Hunters to face three steady but curious faces. It had been so long since the last ride out, the last time we'd all been together. Although there'd been a few conversations back and forth, and I'd seen all of them separately, getting us in the same room was well overdue.

'We're in a bit of a spot, guys,' I explained. 'Money's changed hands, and there's a job to be done.'

'He's been paid before we've even agreed to anything?' asked Jason.

'I've told him he's done wrong,' I explained, 'and it won't happen again. How do you lads feel about it?'

Tommy and Will shrugged, and said they'd follow my lead. If I wanted to go ahead, they were up for it. To my surprise, Jason said no.

'It's too close to home. And he's broken the rules. We should quit while we're ahead.'

Jason had always been the positive one, and for him to back out was serious. It unnerved me. We'd been a tight unit. After a round of handshakes Jason headed off, leaving us with an uncomfortable silence.

'Okay.' I sat forward, taking the impetus. 'I'm up for this, and if you two are, we need a trustworthy replacement.'

'With a decent bike,' added Tommy.

I nodded. 'Let's get together tomorrow, and talk again.'

'I'll have a think,' said Will. 'I might have a name. There's a lad I've known for years through my motorbike track days at Snetterton. He's a really good rider, and I don't think he likes pikeys. I'll sound him out and give him your number.'

The next day Will phoned, explaining that Gerry, the friend from his bike club, had had two trials bikes stolen from his garage, each worth about three grand. He was spitting feathers and had talked of nothing else for weeks. He gave me his number, and I called him up to arrange to meet for a drink.

He walked into the pub with a big grin, shook my hand, and said, 'Will tells me you hate pikeys, too.'

I smiled. He certainly had the right attitude for the job.

'Arseholes broke into my garage and nicked my bikes and all my tools. Lost a bloody fortune, I have.'

We grabbed a couple of pints and sat down in the corner, where he continued his tirade about the thieves.

'I've put a reward out on Facebook and stuff, but not heard a thing.'

'You won't,' I said. 'No Gypsy will dob another in. Those bikes will be up in Cumbria or somewhere for sale by now.'

I wasn't cheering him up much, and we chatted for a bit longer. I was trying to get a feel for the guy, sussing out whether he was all talk or the right candidate for my get-away rider. I looked him hard in the eye a few times while we chatted and I decided he seemed confident enough. Finally I came to the business part of the evening.

'Did Will explain why I wanted to meet you, Gerry?'

Gerry nodded. 'He said I'd get a chance at some pay-back, but didn't give me any details.'

I was pleased that Will had remained tight-lipped about things. I glanced around the quiet pub to check no one was within earshot, then explained what I needed from him, which seemed simple enough. The offer was two hundred and fifty quid to go for a ride. 'Tommy and me will do the hard bit,' I assured him. 'All you have to do is get us back in one piece.'

He lifted his pint, and I lifted mine. We touched glasses and drank to confirm the deal. Then we shook hands and Gerry went home. I texted Will a simple message: 'Your lad G fine,' to which he replied with a smiley face. An emoticon to confirm we had a new co-conspirator.

Although I'd been nervous about recruiting another member, talking with Gerry had revitalized me. I felt a surge of righteousness in what we were doing.

I spent the next few days working out our plan. The method would be the same as before, simply replacing Jason with Gerry. I'd done a couple of drive-bys to confirm exactly where the caravans were, and got busy on Google Earth to scout the area in detail. I worked out the distances involved, the timings, the location of any speed or CCTV cameras. I went through every possible eventuality, every worst-case scenario. Once I was happy with the operation I sent out the coded text to let the boys know to meet up again so we could go through the plan together. Having a new member, I wanted to make doubly certain we all knew what our jobs were.

A few days later we were riding out again. The mission was detailed, and Tommy and I were waiting for the bikes to turn up. We were both laughing at each other's choice of clothes. Again, everything had been sourced from charity shops, and would be destroyed afterwards. Leave no trace.

Will and Gerry pulled up. We donned our helmets and set off. The site was only a hundred yards off the A47, but I'd scouted the perfect lane running close to the caravans that went under the road. The bridge would offer cover for the bikes, and we sat under it for the three minutes of silence, waiting to see if we'd been seen or heard approaching. Not a sound. We left our bags with the bikes and walked up the lane, bottles in hand.

It was a bit further this time to the caravan I'd chosen. Its white side glowed in the moonlight. We paused by a large oak tree, hidden completely under the low-hanging branches.

'Ready, Tom?' I whispered.

'Always,' he whispered back, his teeth shining as he smiled. I'd thought before about Tommy's moral compass. I was driven by a sense of justice, but I think Tommy just enjoyed it. We crept forward, the smell of the petrol-soaked rags thick in my nose. The meadow had tussocks of grass, which made it awkward to move with any speed. We both knew a twisted or broken ankle could prove fatal. Literally.

Once in range Tommy sparked the lighter, and lit the rags. Both fuses burst into flame, and in unison we threw lazy overhands in the direction of the nearest trailer. Tommy was gone before the impact. I stood still.

Boom.

Boom.

The double impact detonated the silence, and the thin sides of the caravan flexed as our missiles hit. The noise was incredible. The glass bottles shattered, the fuel exploded, and there was the loud liquid hiss as the petrol ignited into a sheet of fire. I was transfixed.

'Come on, you prat,' shouted Tommy. He already sounded far away and distant compared to the roaring flames.

I turned in time to see him dart down the lane, clearly visible in the glow from the fireball. I followed as fast as I could. I fell. Fuck. I scrambled up and then fell again.

'Jesus fucking Christ,' I hissed at myself. 'Get up and fucking run.' I commando-rolled over the low bank, trying to stay invisible to the Travellers emerging from the caravans. I could hear dogs barking, men shouting. I crouched and ran. Then I heard the bikes start up, and one pull away. I was close now, legs and arms pumping. When I heard the second bike pull away I swear my heart stopped. I rounded the bend under the bridge to see the red tail-light disappearing up the lane.

Shit. Now I really was fucked. I'd been stranded. The guttural snarl of the powerful bike engines faded into the distance, before I heard a van engine starting up.

Back in the field, men shouted, dogs barked, and two, maybe three more engines fired up and revved out of the field. In my direction. I had moments to hide, and sprinted a hundred yards down the lane and ducked into a hedge, squeezing myself deeper into the mix of blackthorn and brambles.

It was hard going, and the cheap fleece I wore offered no protection against the slicing barbs of the undergrowth. But blind panic pushed me through. I fell out the other side of the hedgerow into a small copse. I had to move, get further from the road. I remembered to breathe and gulped down air, my head dizzy with adrenalin and fear. I crouched and ran, holding my hands in front of my face to protect my eyes from branches and brambles. Every step was a fight against the thorns, and after a few yards I stopped. Only to see two vans drive up the lane. The first at some speed, the second cruising slowly, windows down, powerful torchlight sweeping back and forth through the trees.

I don't think I'd ever felt fear like that. It clawed my guts, making my legs feel weak. I was a dead man if I was caught. The torches they had were for lamping, and rabbits and hares would freeze in the sudden bright light making easy targets for guns or dogs. Now I was the prey.

I had to move. I ran, with only moments before the light played across my back and I'd be seen. And caught.

I half fell into a shallow ditch, no water. Thank God. I lay there, not daring to look over the top. Showing my pale face in the torch beam would be suicidal. I could see the light on the trees around me, illuminating the area as bright as a summer's day. I'd have been seen for sure without that ditch.

Then, thankfully, the lights moved on. The van drove past and the muffled shouts, full of rage and murder, faded. I stayed down. I had no watch, no phone. No method of contacting anyone or getting help. I was stuck. My hands were sore from the hedge, and I had wet scratches on my face.

After a few minutes my breathing returned to normal. How long had I been there? I knew how time could feel distorted in moments of panic or stress. I guessed that I'd been hiding there for anything between five minutes and an hour. I was disoriented, and dehydrated. Silence had reclaimed the woods. I turned over in the damp leaves, smelling that earthy woodland mustiness. I peered over the top of the low ditch that had saved me. No sign of anything. No noise. No movement.

My thinking was that if I couldn't see anyone in the dark then they couldn't see me. Time to move. I crept back to the hedge and paused. I could hear an engine, a motorbike gunning in my direction down the lane. This could easily be friend or foe. Fear took hold and I stayed hidden, shrinking down into the hedge, but keeping a lookout on the road.

It was Will. Good old Will. I recognized his bike as he went past, and I ran out on to the road but he was already a hundred yards past me. He went nearer to the camp, and when I heard him turn around the feeling of relief was physical. My legs felt like rubber, and if I'd needed to run again, I'd have failed. Will saw me and pulled up, a look of shocked concern on his face. I was a right mess. Anyway, no time for sympathy. I leapt on the back and we raced away from the site. We got about a mile away and Will pulled over.

'You okay?' he asked.

'What the fuck happened?' I screamed. 'Where did Gerry go?' I was furious at the fuck-up, the near capture.

'He bottled it. We didn't know until we got to the meet. He turned up on his own. I sent Tommy home with him and came back for you.'

I could hear an edge in Will's voice. He'd brought Gerry into this and it had nearly cost us everything. There was no point taking it out on a good friend. Especially the one who'd come back for me. We rode home in silence and parted with a hug. I've not spoken to Gerry to this day – probably best our paths don't cross again. He's kept quiet about what happened, due to shame, I guess. Not everyone is cut out for action.

The next day the farmer found an almost empty field. The blackened side of a heat-warped caravan faced the road. A few days later a Traveller visited him, leaving threats of vengeance, promises that he'd burn alive the men who torched his caravan. We dismissed it. Nobody knew who we were, and we felt safe enough. But I could feel the bravado slipping. The close shave had affected us all, and maybe it was time to quit.

14

After such a close shave we decided that it'd be wise to call time on torching Traveller camps, and let the dust settle. I was starting to feel more and more uneasy about what we were doing. I'd taken Rhoda out a few times now, and that was creating a real conflict for me. I was very aware of her Romany background, and it was hard to see bad in Gypsies when all I could see was good in her. Listening to her stories about her wider family, the trials and tribulations of Traveller life, was having a definite effect on my feelings about Gypsy folk and their culture. There was a tragic romance to their history, which I was beginning to understand more and more, as well as the clear differences between Romany and Irish Travellers.

Nevertheless, I was still having a running battle, albeit only verbal now, with the Smith clan, but my original motives were fading. Setting caravans alight as a kind of revenge or vigilante justice was one thing, but doing it for money or kicks didn't feel right.

My sympathies were changing. From the initial moral outrage at the stealing and the mess Travellers left behind on abandoned sites, I now wanted to understand the reasons why they chose to live outside society. Well, outside my society. They had their own community, close-knit and connected through blood lines traced back for generations. I knew I'd been lucky not to be caught by either the Gypsies or the police, and I was more than happy to let the past slide into history.

So it was a surprise to get another message from the farmer. He just wanted to meet, he texted. But that text alone broke the rules of communication we'd agreed upon almost two years before. I replied in a noncommittal fashion, suggesting the Larling Angel as a venue. It was well known as one of the best pubs in the area, popular with farmers and the rugby fraternity. Our being there together should raise no eyebrows at all.

I parked and walked into the pub where he was waiting, sitting at a table by the bar. He was even more ruddy-faced than usual, and I could tell he'd been drinking. He launched straight into a Gypsy problem that yet another farmer had.

'Fucking pikeys,' he slurred. 'We'll burn these buggers out, too.'

I cautioned him to be quiet. He was talking loudly, and walls had ears. He became bullish.

'I've already taken the money,' he muttered quietly.

'Are you fucking serious?' I couldn't believe what he'd done after the last conversation we'd had.

'I promised you'd get rid of the bastards for him.'

'Your promise, not mine.'

His point was that as he'd already taken the cash we were obliged to go out again.

'Enough,' I told him. 'We're a man short, and we're lying low after the heat from the last job.'

There was no way I was risking another job he'd set up, and he felt let down. The combination of my temper and his bellyful of beer brought us to an impasse.

'That's not my problem,' he stated.

'And it's not fucking mine, either.'

I got up and walked out of the pub, leaving him sitting there, blank-faced, with half a pint.

It was almost a week before we spoke again. I hadn't wanted to leave things on a bad note, so I drove out to his farm. He met me in the yard, shook my hand, and welcomed me inside. I sat down at the traditional huge farm table, and he put the kettle on.

'I'm sorry, Mike,' he began. 'I've been stupid about this. I should've listened after last time. I guess I just got carried away.'

His honest and simple apology disarmed me. 'Look, it's done now. Let's talk this through and see what we can do.'

After a cup of tea we decided to drive over there and see the lie of the land. I climbed into his Land Rover Discovery, and off we went. It always amazes me how poorly farmers look after their work vehicles and this one was no different. It stank of chicken shit, and the footwells were full of debris, ranging from take-out coffee cups to vermin-poison packaging. There were even some shotgun cartridges rolling about. As we drove I told him in detail just how bad the last trip out had been. It was sinking in just how scared I'd been. Within twenty minutes we were close to the camp, and the farmer slowed down.

The Gypsies had shunted through a gate the farmer had failed to block off. Whenever you see a pile of earth or rubble dumped in a gateway, it's not a lazy farmer: it's a defence to stop Travellers smashing their way into a field.

A scattering of about twenty trailers and caravans were randomly spread over the corner of the meadow. Strings of washing linked the vehicles together. A range of vans, tipper trucks and Range Rovers were parked all around. They'd been there for nearly a month, so the detritus was already piling up. Mounds of tree branches spilt over into heaps of assorted scrap metal. Old prams, fridges, bed frames. Gas bottles of every size and colour. What a shit-hole. Dogs roamed freely around the site, complicating any plan of attack.

And there were children. I counted at least eight youngsters playing throughout the camp. That changed everything.

'There were kids back there,' I said. 'We can't set light to caravans with kids inside.'

He nodded, unusually quiet, and we parked about a mile away in a lay-by.

'Let's just go down there and talk to them,' I suggested. 'There might be a way we can convince them to move on.'

We agreed we'd come back the next day and see if we

could simply talk them into moving on. I didn't hold much hope in a gentle debate shifting a field full of caravans, but it was the only option I was prepared to take. It wasn't just the recurring fear from the last outing: my whole mindset had changed. I was seeing the human side of the Travellers, and who were we to be judge and jury? After the things we'd done, I'd done, we were losing the moral high ground.

On a damp afternoon we drove back to the camp. It wasn't raining, but the sky was dark with cloud, and it suited the mood in the Land Rover. We were sullen the whole way over. The plan was that I'd do the talking, and in my mind I was going over what I'd say.

We parked on a farm track the other side of the field, and got out of the car. My heart was thumping as we walked towards the trailers. I could see the perspiration on the farmer's forehead and upper lip, and realized he was genuinely scared. We'd decided to tape over the number plates on his Discovery, and that was what first caught the men's attention. A collection of Travellers gathered outside, and more filed out of the trailers. We stood still about halfway into the meadow, and three men walked towards us, a gaggle of women and children hanging back.

'What do you want?' The first one spoke with an Irish lilt in his voice.

'No trouble,' I replied, trying to keep my voice steady. My left knee was shaking. I could feel it. It'd always been my tell, a signal that things were going to kick off. 'How long are you staying here?'

'What's it to you?' he answered quietly, and stared directly into my eyes. I refused to look away and held his gaze.

After the frosty greeting I wasted no time. I'd rehearsed a clever speech, but all the words went out of the window, and I slowly but clearly explained that there was a strong likelihood of fires in these fields. 'And there might be fires again,' I hinted.

I was way off script, but I was just reacting to the situation. We stood there staring at each other. The tension was like a stretched piano wire. About to snap. My threat was clear. There was no chance these guys hadn't heard about the other burnings. The Travelling community might not have talked to the police but they'd surely talked to each other. I glanced at the farmer. He had his poker face on, but I knew he was scared.

'Best you folk move on,' he advised. 'No need for any accidents.'

Two younger lads had joined the first three, and we were badly outnumbered. These guys didn't look happy.

'Let's go,' I said, seeing a flicker of relief cross the farmer's face. We walked backwards towards his car, maintaining eye contact.

And they followed.

Bollocks.

I could smell the wet grass, and hear crows in the distance over the dull rumble of passing traffic. Everything seemed to slow down. We reached his car and I heard him open the door. I turned around in time to see him pull out a twelve-bore shotgun.

'Don't be a twat,' I warned.

He put the stock to his shoulder and raised the barrel.

Oh, sweet Jesus, what was he thinking? The faces of the Travellers hardly flinched. They'd seen guns before.

I froze. I knew the farmer was scared, and scared people do stupid things. The Gypsies had stopped about twenty yards away, and the farmer was staring down two barrels at the group of men, a twitchy finger on the trigger. I could even see the whiteness in his joints, the pressure with which he was holding the gun. But he surely wouldn't, would he?

He pulled the trigger.

The crack of that shot sounded like the sky was falling in. The bang was deafening. Pigeons and other birds flew up into the overcast sky.

Then silence.

The smell of the discharged cartridge drifted over the roof of the car. The farmer had blasted lead shot a few feet above their heads. I'd flinched, and the Gypsies hadn't. Luckily he still had a cartridge in the chamber, or they'd have rushed us.

'Fucking go,' I told him.

He scrambled round and climbed into the passenger seat, not closing the door, but holding the gun out beside the windscreen, ready to fire again. The engine roared into life, and I pulled away, leaving a group of livid men staring after us. I backed down the track, aware that his door was wide open. Nobody followed. They'd realized he was a loose cannon, and the chance of getting lead pellets at speed held them back. He brought the gun inside, broke the mechanism to make it safe, and closed the door. He also reloaded the spent chamber.

'Just in case,' he gasped, between snatched breaths. He was almost hyperventilating.

Then the argument started. 'What the fuck did you think you were doing?'

'I should've aimed a bit fucking lower.'

'You could've killed someone!' I shouted, reversing out of the gate and on to the narrow lane. 'We could've been fucking killed!' I was furious, and went into a rant. 'What the fuck were you thinking? You stupid bloody idiot.' I powered the Land Rover through the bends, and accelerated away from the camp. 'Anything could have happened. What if they'd pulled a gun? You do know they have guns, don't you?'

He stayed silent, his hands shaking.

'If any one of them had a camera, or a phone, we are royally fucked.'

'I'm sorry, Mike,' he said. 'I just lost it. I thought they were going to grab us.'

He was still trembling. It proved again that taking action was not for the faint-hearted.

And now we were marked men, for sure. How had I allowed that to happen? The whole idea had been a bad one from the start. What would the consequences be?

There would be a price to pay for today's disaster.

15

After my farmer friend had done his John Wayne act, and fired a volley of shot over the heads of a Gypsy clan, word got around. My town grew smaller and smaller. The fall-out from the burnings and the on-going battle with the Smiths, the thieves I'd caught red-handed in my yard, had taken the shine off living in Ledburgh. I was feeling more and more certain that I was a hunted man, and the net was closing.

Although the last group of Travellers had moved on the next day, they'd left a repeat of their original chilling message with the farmer's friend that they would find us and burn us alive.

The shotgun incident had scared me, so it must have shaken them too. And witnessing the farmer's lack of control had made up my mind. I wouldn't be going out again. We talked it through and I made it clear: if he took any more money he'd be the one visiting the camps, alone. And there was no way he'd put himself through that again.

Admittedly I was on mental and physical alert, but the atmosphere in Ledburgh felt strange. The community had reclaimed the town centre, police were regularly out on patrol, and the yobs were rarely seen. But something was wrong. There was an undercurrent of tension. It was hard to pin down but it felt like the troublemakers were just biding their time. Waiting for the police presence to reduce or move on.

It was around this period of relative quiet that I walked into the wine bar to hear raucous laughter.

'Mike,' said Matthew, a local electrician, 'you won't believe this.' He had to pause to gather his breath as he was laughing so much.

'What's up?' I was grinning already – their laughter was infectious.

'One of the Smiths has been arrested for shagging a horse,' he exclaimed, with real shock in his voice.

'You're kidding.'

'Honest to God,' he swore. 'I was on the estate when the police cars raced up there. Everyone saw it.'

'Everyone saw it?'

Matthew told me how one of the Smiths had walked into a field where they kept a few typical Gypsy ponies. There was a new office building beside the paddock next to the train tracks, which had been fitted with mirrored glass windows. As he couldn't see anyone he thought nobody could see him. How wrong he was. While horrified staff looked on, and one of the busiest trains of the morning went by on the main line from Norwich to London, he'd simply cracked on with his business at the rear end of the pony. The police and the RSPCA had taken a combined total of over a hundred phone calls from passengers and office workers, saying they were watching a guy shag a horse in broad daylight.

'That can't be true,' I said, utterly stunned.

'You'll see,' said Matthew, going back to his pint.

Sure enough, the lurid details emerged in the following days. One of the family had been arrested and was charged with bestiality. I already knew the stories about the Smiths' drug-dealing, petty thefts, burglaries and other criminal activities, but this was unreal.

It obviously wasn't just that sick act which made me think differently about the town, but it didn't help. Living in Ledburgh had lost its appeal for me. I'd made some great friends, Saracen was going from strength to strength and the wine bar was thriving, but I didn't feel comfortable there any more. Apart from the threats made by the Travellers after the first caravan burnings, and the shotgun encounter, I had no evidence I was being hunted. But was I just paranoid?

It was time to move away for a while.

Little did I know that I would soon be living exactly as those I'd once attacked.

As a child I'd been a regular visitor to the Peak District. My parents used to take us camping on a dairy farm at the base of Win Hill. We never missed milking time, and I loved watching the farmer bring the herd in through the gates to the dairy sheds. Playing on the local parks through the school holidays, I'd made friends at a young age and was still in touch with them twenty years later. Once you make the effort to say hello, there's a natural open streak in northern folk, and lasting bonds are formed.

When I was a young adult I took a girlfriend up there one weekend to give her a break from my endless obsession with rugby. Standing on top of Mam Tor at two in the afternoon I spotted some rugby posts in the valley below, just outside Castleton, where tiny figures jogged up and down getting ready for a game. It was too much for me to bear. I climbed down the hill and ran off towards the rugby pitch. By the time I got there they'd kicked off on the muddiest ground I'd ever seen. After a while one of the Hope Valley lads came off injured, covered from head to toe with thick, cold mud.

'Have you not got any subs?' I asked. He shook his head and walked towards their changing rooms. I followed him in and asked what size boots he had on.

By the time my poor girlfriend had found the pitch I was playing on, I was hardly recognizable in the mud. I loved it. It was the start of a strong relationship with the club, and the end of my relationship with the young lady. Now, years later, with a successful engineering business, I was a proud sponsor of that great little social side. I played for the team whenever I was in Derbyshire, and when a friend mentioned that a house was coming up for auction I asked for more information. It was semi-detached, on the very edge of Castleton in the heart of the valley. I knew exactly where it was and thought it was perfect. I tracked down the owner's number through a few friends and made the call. The owner was happy to accept my bid and we shook hands the day before the auction. I was now a happy resident of Hope Valley.

I was well aware that moving away meant I wouldn't see Rhoda again, but things had cooled between us. Our last few conversations had felt awkward. I was still infatuated with her, and every time I saw her my heart would race, but the atmosphere of our relationship had definitely changed. In my paranoia I wondered if she'd heard a rumour about the caravan burnings, or was just wary of my conflict with the Smiths. Although that family didn't mix with Tony and Rhoda's, they were still Travellers, so my constant griping about them might have put her off. I also had seriously mixed feelings about some of the things we'd done. There was real guilt once the self-professed justification had worn thin, and I felt that the farmers had used us to solve a problem they'd helped to cause in the first place. My sense of bravado had allowed them to use me, like a pawn in a game of chess, doing their dirty work while they sat back. This conflict of emotions had affected my time with Rhoda. No relationship can be built on a foundation of lies and deception. And I knew in my heart that if I was to be open with her, confess what I'd been involved in, she'd never talk to me again. I was taking the coward's way out by letting it slide with no real conversation between us. It would cost me dear in the future.

So, I made my plans to leave the area without involving Rhoda. Although my business was based in Norfolk, I had a really good management team in place at Saracen, and we talked through the logistics of my satellite directorship plan. I could go to sites from Derbyshire as easily as from East Anglia, so things should be able to carry on as before.

On one of my visits back to the wine bar I got into a conversation with Andy, an older friend, who was a regular lunchtime customer. He asked me to sit at his table away from everyone at the bar. He was famously close-lipped, but over the years we'd forged a genuine respect for each other.

'How's life up in Derbyshire?' he asked.

I replied with enthusiasm, telling him about the six pubs in my village, the hill walking, the rugby. Life was good in the valley.

Andy nodded, looked around the bar, then spoke quietly: 'You might be interested in some recent chatter around town.'

I felt a shiver, and recalled the old saying about someone walking over your grave.

'What do you mean, chatter?'

'Some Travellers were in last week, asking who owned the wine bar, and who'd organized the meeting at the Park Hotel.'

He was actually whispering to me now. This was a nightmare, but I kept a blank face. 'Why would Travellers be asking after me?'

'No idea.' He shrugged. 'Just thought you should know.'

I could tell he had an inkling of what they were after, but Andy was sharp enough not to expand further.

The bad news sat in my gut for days. Even in Derbyshire it affected my sleep. So I made the sad decision to sell the wine bar. I was miles away, anyway, and the whole point of buying it was to live in the flat above and have my own regular, and very local, drinking hole. I was no longer there to be a front-of-house presence, which was always bad news for any bar or pub. And from what Andy had told me it was probably a good job. I'd be a sitting duck if I really was a target.

After I'd come to terms with selling the business, I made some calls and went back for what would be my last night at the wine bar. My plan was to invite some close friends, and although I'd already moved away, there was going to be a sort of leaving party. I tried contacting Rhoda to see if she could come but got no reply. I was too busy with work and trying to get a good price for the bar to dwell on it, but the lack of contact left a nagging hole in my excitement for the night ahead.

That afternoon I signed papers to appoint an agent for the sale. Word had already got round it was on the market, and he indicated there was early interest. That set my mind at ease, so I went to the flat and got ready for what would be my final evening in Ledburgh.

I'd asked the boys to join me, as I couldn't see any harm in corralling the gang for one more night. This would be our last chance to drink together for a long time. Gerry stayed away, although he'd made it clear there was no issue, and Jason had returned to the fold for one more booze-up.

'So this is really it, then?' asked Jason. 'You're moving up there permanently?'

'Yes, mate,' I replied, feeling a bit melancholy. 'After the Park Hotel meeting I'm a marked man. It's been a good run, and so far, touch wood, we're clear of any payback.'

The conversation steered on to other things – Hope Valley rugby club, and how many good pubs were within walking distance of my new home.

Soon the bar filled with friends and colleagues from Saracen. I'd mentioned to a few folk that this would be my farewell, and the topic of the Travellers and the attacks didn't surface. At least for that night. It became a cracking party, lots of laughs and drinks, and I woke with a thick head the next morning.

Within a few weeks the wine bar was sold. No surprise in the quick deal as it was a popular venue, but it felt like the end of an era, and I was sad because I had some great memories from my time there. However, the overwhelming sense of relief at closing the trail off from the Gypsies was more important.

With the wine bar gone, I could focus all my energies on the engineering business. I was working hard, running a project in Hull and driving around the country to see customers. It was good news all round as Sam had proposed to his long-term girlfriend and the wedding was announced for the summer. He had asked me to share best-man duties with David, another long-term friend and regular in the wine bar. David had been out to Thailand with us to help with the electrical-control side of things and done a fine job.

'You're in trouble now, Sam,' I told him, 'with me and Dave planning your stag trip.'

Sam laughed. He knew he was in safe hands. The guest list included the usual suspects from Saracen and a few male relatives of Sam and Paula, his wife-to-be. We headed for Newquay and landed in the single dingiest hotel you could imagine before a rowdy piss-up around the town. The only damp note was one lad breaking his leg jumping over a bench on the first night there. He spent the rest of the trip in hospital nearby. At the wedding I made a reference to it during my joint-best-man's speech, joking that a bouncer at a brothel had warned that anyone getting too kinky would be dragged outside and have their leg busted. At that point I paused and looked at the poor lad sitting at the back with his cast elevated on a chair. It got a good laugh as folk twigged what I was hinting at.

On the actual day of the wedding I felt oddly detached from my friends. I'd moved away and had so many secrets from them. A whole second life I couldn't share. It confirmed to me that my future was in Derbyshire where I was enjoying a new start in life. I loved my new home, and the village was perfect for me, surrounded by beautiful hills, and friendly pubs vibrant with tourists and locals.

I became more and more involved with the rugby club, and we started to enjoy real success, both on the field and off, organizing some buzzing socials as well as gaining promotion in the local league. To embed myself even deeper into the Derbyshire community I decided to buy a dog.

My family had always owned German Pointers. They were great gun dogs and well suited to the waterways and hedgerows of Norfolk. Benson, who was now living with my brother, out of the way of any vengeful drug dealers, was also a Pointer so I searched online for a local breeder. I ended up driving to a farm in the Wirral that had a great reputation for their breeding kennels. On arrival I was shown through to an enclosed lawn to view a litter that would be available in three weeks' time. On my way across the grass some older puppies were tumbling about, enjoying the sunshine and playing with each other. Apart from one. A single puppy, completely brown except for his chest and his two front paws, made a beeline for me. He clamped himself to the hem of my jeans and refused to let go.

'This one's lively.' I was disarmed by the unspeakably cute bundle hanging off my leg.

'He's part of an older litter,' said the breeder. 'He's not sold yet. You could take him today, if you like?'

I'd planned to view the more recent litter and come back after the eight-week weaning period. But as I picked him up and we made eye contact for the first time I knew he was my dog.

'I think he chose you.'

She was right. Halfway home I settled on the name Alfie. And I couldn't have wished for a better companion. My old friend Stephen and I would go on to enjoy hundreds of walks and wanderings, Alfie bounding about. For the first few months he'd sit in my rucksack after a few miles' hiking to protect his joints. We must have looked a strange sight wandering down from the hills and arriving at a pub with him licking my ears from his elevated position on my back. He soon outgrew that rucksack, but never his puppy-like joy of bounding through the fields and over the hills of Derbyshire.

Ledburgh and all its troubles, the Travellers and all the consequences, seemed a world away. Life was good, and I couldn't remember being happier.

16

One of my main passions in life is hill walking. From those first family trips into the countryside to my teenage adventures across Europe and beyond, there's nothing better than striding across some windswept peaks. My love of Hope Valley was in part due to the nearby heather-topped moorland that made up the Dark Peak area, and trekking beside the crystal-clear streams that cut through the dales of White Peak. Since I'd got Alfie I had another incentive to get out on a daily basis. Watching him bound through the heather was a joy, and his obvious pleasure inspired my own. We'd often head out for the whole day on a route dotted with rural ale houses, returning to Castleton at dusk where I'd finish off the hike by calling into a couple of pubs in the village before heading home.

This sedate lifestyle made me realize how much pressure I'd been under before I'd moved there. Building up Saracen to its current level, I'd joked about working eight days a week. I'd usually go from the office to running the wine bar, and although it was a different business, it still carried responsibilities, and I'd never really had any time off in years. Add to that the issues with the Gypsies, and my life had been non-stop.

It was strange how all of that seemed so far away now.

Almost as if it had never happened. But it had. There were nights when my sleep would be disturbed by bad dreams. Images of burning caravans, blurring speed on motorbikes, angry confrontations. I could feel an undercurrent of unease hidden deep inside despite my new location and lifestyle. I'd effectively blocked it out of my daily life.

Until an episode took place in which I was forced to confront that history directly.

I was out in the Derbyshire countryside, walking Alfie through some meadows, when it felt like somebody had struck me on the back of the head with a cricket bat.

I dropped to one knee as if I was about to propose to the dog. Head in hands I looked around, convinced someone was there, poised to attack again.

No. I was alone. In the middle of a field. The pain was so intense and so focused I felt nauseous. I stayed there for a few minutes, waving Alfie away, his curiosity bouncing him into me a number of times. Even though he was a puppy he knew something was wrong and paused, head cocked to the side.

'Jeez, Alfie. That hurt, that really hurt.'

I often found myself talking to him, and wondered if it was a sign of friendship or madness. Either way, he encouraged me to gather myself up and limp home, one hand pressed against my forehead to try to relieve the pain. It faded slowly that evening, but it really shook me up.

The headache struck three more times over the next week, and I was genuinely scared of the intensity. Without

144

warning I'd get a sharp pain in the back of my skull followed by dizziness and nausea. The fifth and sixth headaches caused me to pass out. The pain was too much to bear. I can remember falling to the ground, thinking I was dying.

I'd already spoken to Stephen about the headaches, and they had dominated our recent rambles, the walks being cut shorter because of my concerns. After many years of local rugby and Murrayfield trips, to see his beloved Scotland play, we had a strong friendship and understanding of each other. He knew I wasn't swinging a leg and shared my worry about the cause of the headaches.

It was just after the sixth episode, as I was coming round in my house, that Stephen let himself in with a greeting.

Finding me in such a muddle he rushed me straight to the Royal Hallamshire Hospital in Sheffield, where I was admitted for tests. He stayed with me for a while but when it became obvious I was being admitted he left me with assurances he'd collect Alfie and look after him. Stephen and I had been on many walks with Alfie as our much fitter companion, and there was a shared affection between them so I knew he'd be spoilt rotten. Meanwhile I underwent every test available. Scans and blood samples were taken. It was a strange, almost dreamlike time. I felt safe in the hospital and, for the first time in years, genuinely relaxed. It was as if I was floating in and out of reality.

I was very aware of being isolated from most of the

folk in my life. My family were back in Norfolk, as were most of my old friends. The friends who visited me during my stay were from Hope Valley, with no connection to the past. I was also aware of a kind of anonymity in the massive NHS machine: nobody knew me or my history. These things all added to a sense of security during my extended stay there. I was sleeping like a baby through the nights and happily dozing most of the day. My batteries must have been at such a low level that I hadn't noticed or had time to recharge.

I had a lumbar puncture, a procedure similar to the epidural with which some pregnant women are familiar. In a foetal position my vertebrae were positioned to allow a thick needle to pass between the bones. A fine needle was then pushed into the spine via the first needle. This allowed a sample of spinal fluid to be extracted.

Red blood cells were found in my spinal fluid, which was bad news. It indicated an aneurysm had caused a leak, and this had been the reason for my headaches. The specialist told me they're called 'thunderclap' headaches in the medical profession, and I thought that was pretty apt, considering the intense pain.

I ended up staying in hospital for three weeks, most of which I spent dozing or undergoing tests. I bonded with my consultant after swapping rugby stories, and we also shared a love of the Peak District. I'd described my work regime to him and he made it clear that, in his opinion, my aneurysm was stress-related. Bear in mind that I hadn't told him I was a wanted man.

During my second week in hospital I received a text from an unknown number. It simply read: *Hi, heard you were in hospital, hope you're okay? Be good to catch up sometime.*

I replied: *Thank you for the kind wishes, apologies but my phone hasn't recognized your number, who is this?*

At this point it was a pretty neutral text, and could have been male or female.

Rhoda xx.

My stomach flipped. It had been so long since our last contact, back in Ledburgh. My number had remained the same because of work, but hers had changed. I quickly worked out how many texts I'd sent to her old number. Dozens. All unanswered, and now I knew why. We started a dialogue of polite chat, catching up on news, my new home, Alfie, among other things. It seemed that her life had plodded along in contrast to my crazy pace of change. Moving from Ledburgh to Norwich was her biggest event since our period of dating. I was sitting watching the phone, waiting for a fresh text, enjoying being back in contact.

In one of the few photos she sent she looked as stunning as ever. I realized how much I'd missed her being around.

Ultimately, with the aneurysm, I'd been exceptionally lucky not to have further complications such as stroke symptoms. When you're laid up in hospital it offers you long periods of time to think things through, and I decided I needed a change, and a bigger change than just moving house. I decided to take a huge step back from

Saracen, and leave the running of the business to my partners. My consultant had advised me to eliminate as much stress from my life as possible to avoid more trouble with the aneurysm. Advice I intended to follow. Over the following months, I 'enjoyed' a series of lumbar punctures to monitor the presence of red blood cells. Thankfully, there were none.

A few days after I was discharged from hospital, I drove down to meet with Sam and Colin, the two managers who were running Saracen on a day-to-day basis. After the usual joshing around I explained I had a plan to hand over the business. Starting that year they'd receive ten per cent each year until they owned it outright. We had a full order book and the future seemed to be assured. There were no other engineering firms in the industry offering such a complete service.

Meanwhile, I had weekly lumbar punctures for the first month after my discharge, and the good news was that the red blood cell count had gone down to trace elements. As long as I avoided stressful situations I should be fine. Still, I needed a job to occupy my time. Something less hectic than CEO of my own business.

I'd always daydreamed about running guided walks in the Peak District. Designing routes and investing in a minibus would be easier on the nerves than managing multi-million-pound engineering projects. Years before, I'd drafted a business plan for a guided-walks holiday project, which I'd intended to submit to Virgin via their company web page. The original idea was to have a fleet of vehicles collecting folk from all over the country and ferrying them to youth-hostel-style digs in the beautiful countryside. The days out would be followed by evenings in local pubs, all chauffeur-driven. It seemed like a winner, but the Virgin submission process was so long-winded I lost heart and shelved the idea. Now I revisited the project with the intention of running it myself. I traded in my Range Rover for a seventeen-seater mini-bus and set about designing the walks around my area.

For a while it was a distraction from my health issues, but the fact is I never really gave it my full attention. A business is bound to fail if you don't give it everything you've got. In the end the minibus was used mostly by Hope Valley Rugby Club, and the idea just petered out.

That whole episode had shown me just how fragile life was, and I was determined to live it to the full from now on. Was I on borrowed time? I certainly felt grateful for my good fortune, and with a brighter and more optimistic outlook, I was enjoying a full recovery. I'd chatted to Rhoda regularly on the phone, and we'd always ended up laughing and talking typical nonsense. We even mentioned meeting up next time I returned to Norfolk.

17

A great social event took place every year at Norwich RFC. It was called 'Back to Norwich' and involved a reunion of veteran players forming a scratch team to play against the current development squad. It was such a simple but effective idea, and not to be missed. The banter in the changing rooms before the game was typical of rugby friends. Despite not seeing each other for months, sometimes years at a time, that special bond was still strong. I always felt especially grateful to be invited back as I'd left the club acrimoniously after a disagreement with the management.

When I'd first arrived at the club we fielded up to seven teams every Saturday. Then the sport turned professional and outfits such as Norwich, with delusions of grandeur and a bit of quick cash, went bonkers. Without need they started paying first-team players and rewarding them with suits and sponsored cars. What they failed to appreciate was that the entire squad loved the club, and would have played for them regardless of any reward. All they achieved was the alienation of the lower teams. Why should they be paying subs and putting money over the bar when the club was tipping it down the nearest drain as fast as possible? Officials had openly said that they'd be happy running a one-team club, with reserves and a development side. No time for social teams.

After a very public argument about the future of social rugby, I left and set up Apache RFC, a side made up of half a dozen veteran players and guys from down the pub. And I mean literally from out of the pub. Guys who hadn't played since school, or had never played at all. As we had no ground we always played away from home. But we invariably took huge numbers of supporters with us so the hosting club had a good take over the bar. It was a great success for the two years I ran it and proved my point that, given the right format, there was plenty of life left in social rugby. We'd generated more than a hundred new players who went on to join local clubs.

I combined my visit back to Norfolk with a couple of days in the office at Saracen. It was good to see things were going really well, but it did make feel a bit, well, obsolete.

Still, I had the rugby to enjoy. As in previous years, the veterans had the edge on the youngsters. The generous passing created some lovely flowing rugby, and the older heads made the game look easy. Despite the greater speed and fitness of the younger lads, the veterans were smarter, moving the ball into the open spaces while the headstrong opposition crashed into rucks and tackles. After the match came the highlight of the day: a few well-earned beers. We traded stories and caught up on news. We were a crowd of smiling faces, and after we'd drunk enough beer to drown a bull elephant it was decided we should head into Norwich city centre.

Back in my early twenties I'd run a bar in the city, one of the busiest venues on the nightlife scene. We'd packed it out every evening, so I was viewed by the lads as someone with a bit of inside knowledge when it came to going out in town, and I still had firm friends among the management and staff who worked the pubs and clubs.

We headed for the edge of the main drag, sank a few pints in some smaller boozers, then landed in a huge Wetherspoons called the Glasshouse. The atmosphere was electric, and it was one of those nights when everyone was laughing and joking, broad smiles on all our faces. I thought things couldn't get any better.

Then she walked into the bar.

It was as if someone had clicked a pause button on the laughter.

For a moment the noise seemed to subside. They were all staring at her. Rhoda had walked through the door and at least a hundred guys' jaws had hit the floor. She was stunning. Her long brunette hair framed a face of perfection – full lips, dark eyes above those sharp cheekbones. Bare shoulders, slim waist, and legs that balanced gracefully on dangerous heels. Then she smiled, and the angels sang.

She was smiling at me.

'Fuck's sake, would you look at that!' said Ian, a veteran winger tempted out of retirement to relive past glories earlier that afternoon.

'I am,' I replied, still staring. 'I know her.'

She looked immaculate. She walked through the crowded pub, like Moses through the Red Sea, people shuffling out of her way as if she was royalty. And she was, in her own way. A Gypsy princess.

'So, here you are then.' She smiled, eyes sparkling with intrigue.

'It's been a while, Rhoda. How are you?'

Although we'd talked on the phone about meeting in Norwich I hadn't thought she'd actually turn up. And not walking in there like that, on her own. She'd always been confident, assured in her looks, and that she was out of bounds to guys in general: her father and brother's fearsome reputations offered her a sense of security. Gypsy patriarchs are highly protective of their daughters, and Rhoda was no different. But that was back in Ledburgh. This was Norwich, where her family were unknown.

And the looks on my mates' faces. They couldn't believe I was talking with a girl who looked like that. Nor could I, if I'm honest. There are times in life that stay in your memory to be relived and enjoyed over and over again. And the next four hours I spent with Rhoda was one of them. I totally ignored all my rugby team, but no one complained on the night or afterwards. Nobody with a pulse would have acted differently. I bought us some drinks and we sat down away from the bar.

'So how are you?' I asked again, unable to break eye contact. I was drowning in those dark eyes. And her smile didn't falter. She was enjoying the effect she was having on me.

'I'm okay,' she said. 'Life could be better, but I'm okay.' She explained that she'd moved away from Ledburgh and was now living in Norwich.

'Well, I don't miss Ledburgh,' I said. 'That's for sure. But I do miss you.'

It was true. I hadn't realized my true feelings for her, which had resurfaced so strongly as she'd walked into the bar. My stomach felt light, despite the drinking, and I felt sober, which was crazy considering how much I'd consumed. She reached for my hand.

'I've missed you as well,' she said, holding my eyes with hers. It was a charged moment. I could literally feel the sparks flying.

We spent the rest of the evening wandering from bar to bar. At which point we started holding hands, I couldn't say. It just happened, and it felt so right. We caught up on all our news. I had to be careful not to reveal some of my reasons for leaving the area. I was fighting the alcohol and a bizarre urge to tell her everything. But my attraction to her was so strong it was easy to forget Rhoda was a pure Romany Gypsy. It was an understatement to say she wouldn't be happy with some of the things I'd done. She knew of my troubles with the Smiths in Ledburgh, but she didn't like them anyway. No real Gypsies did. They brought shame on the community they claimed to be part of, and they were an embarrassment to genuine Travellers. So I skirted around a few issues, but told Rhoda how I'd settled in Derbyshire.

That same feeling of inner conflict was still inside me. The drink was close to letting me unburden myself, and being totally honest with her, a beautiful Gypsy girl. But I couldn't do it. My oath of silence with my friends and the slightest chance of her walking away were too much to overcome. It remained a secret between us, a dark secret I'd have to live with.

'It's perfect up there,' I said. 'I'm in the most amazing village – people are so friendly and the six pubs are always busy. Within half an hour you can be in Manchester or Sheffield.'

Rhoda had always been a lover of the big cities – her style and presence seemed suited for the bigger stage, not tucked away in rural isolation. I felt as if I was making a sales pitch. But she was loving it, soaking up every detail of where I now lived, and the life I was enjoying. By the end of the night I'd invited her up to visit for a weekend. And she'd agreed – I hadn't harangued or had to persuade her: she'd actually agreed to come up and see me. I couldn't believe what was happening. The thoughts going through my mind, the sense of euphoria, were making me feel light-headed. Our last hour together we spent kissing and staring at each other. The rest of the world had ceased to exist. It felt incredible.

I walked Rhoda to her taxi. 'I don't know what just happened tonight,' I whispered in her ear, holding her close.

'I know,' she replied. 'But I like it. I like it a lot.'

She squeezed me tightly, then gracefully slid into the

waiting car. I closed the door and watched her taxi drive away. I stood there for at least five minutes after the vehicle had disappeared, the grin on my face making my cheeks hurt. Was this really happening? Oh, yes, it was. And it felt so good. This had been one of the best evenings of my life, the effects of which were about to transform everything.

18

It was pretty clear that the main cause of my illness was stress. It was also obvious that most of it had been self-inflicted. The lack of delegation in my business over the years had taken its toll. Only after a decade did I realize that if my staff did something in a slightly different way that didn't make it the wrong way. The end result was the same: the clients were always happy and the invoice would be paid. My obsession with controlling every job had come at a heavy cost. And it was stupid. I was paying good money to good engineers who were more than capable of doing it themselves. And now I had no choice but to go from one extreme to the other, from being ever-present on every project to virtually retiring.

The consultant had instructed me to engage in some relaxing hobbies. Burning Gypsy caravans was not on the list of serene pastimes so I tried my hand at painting.

I bought half a dozen blank canvases, and a bottle each of black and white paint. I'd always enjoyed Banksy-style images so had a go at copying a few of his classics. To my surprise, never having touched a brush in forty years, I discovered I had a talent. I could paint. The style was basic but the results looked pretty good.

When I sent Rhoda photos of my work she initially

thought I was winding her up. She simply didn't believe I was the artist, which I took as a compliment. We'd been in regular contact since that night in Norwich, texting all day and at least one phone call every night.

'So, what do you really think?' I asked, after getting a thumbs-up emoji by text.

'It's good. Really good. You should try to sell them. I bet you'd get fifty quid.' Rhoda was always looking for the money angle, a chance to turn a pound. She was a natural-born trader, like most Gypsies, and everything she owned or bought was with a view to selling it on at a profit. She hardly ever cut the tags out of clothes despite wearing them. She would either return or resell them.

I took her advice and set up a page on Facebook. I'd already posted photos of the paintings on my personal page and the feedback was great. Enquiries to buy my pictures came in, and I even sold some. I couldn't believe folk would buy my work to hang in their homes, but they did, and it felt fantastic to be appreciated in that way.

I tried my hand at portraits: the first few were a disaster but I could see potential.

I rang Rhoda and offered to paint her.

'Yes.' She laughed. 'If you care about me you really should.'

'You'll have to come up here for a sitting,' I said, with a smile. She knew I worked from photos so the invitation to visit was nothing to do with her portrait.

'How far is it up there?' Rhoda asked.

'Three and a half hours, I reckon.' I didn't just reckon,

I knew full well. I'd done that journey so many times over the years I could have driven it blindfolded. 'When are you thinking?'

My heart was thumping for obvious reasons.

'How about next weekend?' she asked.

'It's a date,' I replied, unable to keep the excitement out of my voice.

All week I made preparations, stocking nice food in the fridge, buying fancy bottles of wine, and tidying up the place as best I could. I was still working on the house but some parts were almost finished. It looked pretty good. But was it good enough? And why was I worrying so much?

When Rhoda stepped out of her car I knew why I was trying to make such an impression. The hug we had on her arrival, the cheeky kiss, the holding hands as I walked her up the path: this was happening. I could feel it. And I could tell Rhoda felt the same.

'How was your drive?' I asked, lifting her incredibly heavy suitcase inside. She never travelled light.

'More than four hours. I nearly turned round and went back.' She was teasing, trying to get a reaction. The stupid thing was, I did feel something at the thought of her not arriving. I didn't like it. But here she was, as beautiful as ever, and making a big fuss of Alfie, who'd come to see who was hugging his boss.

'Do you want to freshen up or head into the village for a drink?'

'I'll just put my face on,' she replied, 'and change into something nice.'

To me, she looked perfect. I'm sure she'd pulled her car over ten minutes before arriving to check herself out. To make an impression, I hoped.

Half an hour later we walked up to the Cheshire Cheese, the nearest pub to my house and my firm favourite. Faye, one of two daughters who helped run the pub, greeted us in her piss-take Norfolk accent. 'All roight, Moike?'

Larger than life, always ready with a smile and some banter, she was an aspiring actress waiting for her big break. In the meantime she entertained us in her parents' pub.

'This is Rhoda,' I said. They smiled and started chatting. Rhoda ordered a Disaronno and Coke, and I left them to it to say hello to a few friends at the bar. As we left an hour later Faye made us promise to call in again and we headed up to the village centre. That weekend we visited all six pubs in Castleton, multiple times. All of my friends, old and new, went out of their way to make Rhoda feel welcome. I was just weeks away from my fortieth birthday and asked Rhoda if she'd come back up and help me host the party at my house. It sounded like an excuse, but she readily agreed.

The weekend was full of romance and deep conversations about the future. Constantly holding hands. Constantly laughing. We'd driven up to Mam Tor car park and wandered up the peak to see the breathtaking views. I was reminded of standing on that same spot many years before, and running down the hill to play rugby. I told Rhoda the story, pointing out the posts far below. She called me a thoughtless pig for leaving the poor girl up there, then smiled. 'But I'm glad you did. I wouldn't be here otherwise.'

I was sad to see her car pull away on Monday. It had been a wonderful few days.

Rhoda had helped me set up the Facebook page for my painting, and it seemed I had the chance of a nice little sideline there, so I stuck at it. As far as relaxing went it was just the tonic. I could feel the tension easing out of my mind. My health was good and the paintings were a large part of it. I sat with the consultant and told him of the success I was enjoying with the art. 'I'd never touched a brush before,' I laughed, 'and now I'm a selling artist.'

The consultant explained how another patient of his, who'd suffered a similar aneurysm, had discovered on his recovery that he could speak fluent Spanish. He had insisted that, prior to his illness, he couldn't say a word in any foreign language. Somewhere in our brains lie knowledge and skills that remain hidden until the grey matter gets a jolt. I wasn't complaining: not only was I making a full recovery but I had a new skill to boot.

After hours of concentration and focus, I finished the portrait of Rhoda and stepped back to look at it properly. I know I'm biased, but I'd nailed it. She was beautiful, and this was an image that captured her perfectly. Maybe it was the extra care that went into it, but it remains one of my best ever paintings.

19

One of the long-term projects I'd worked on at Saracen was to reduce costs in halal processing. I'd invested countless hours in studying halal and understanding the reasons behind it, learning that animals killed using the method decreed in the Koran must be healthy, blessed with a prayer during the slaughter, and have all their blood drained from the carcass. Many people react badly as soon as they hear the word 'halal'. 'Dirty Muslim bastards,' or 'Cruel religious nuts,' were common openers on the subject. As the years went by, and I gained more knowledge on the subject, I found myself arguing on behalf of halal slaughter.

'All of our chickens used to be killed by hand,' I'd explain to those who'd actually listen, 'until the big retailers wanted to streamline the process for money, not animal welfare.'

The way we killed our chickens on behalf of the supermarkets was a disgrace. Individual slaughter, such as that required by halal or kosher custom, involved far less suffering. The limiting factor in the process was delay in the slaughter room. To speed it up and create a cheaper supply chain, mechanization had been rolled out, driven by the big supermarkets so they could reduce their costs. Stunning was then introduced, not for animal welfare, but to speed up the line and make the birds easier to hang on the shackles.

I'd attended meetings at Westminster with MPs, and even been to Brussels to talk on the subject. It was a strange contrast to my hidden life battling with the Travellers. I loved moving in those circles, engaging and debating with highly educated and powerful people. I realized again that living my double life had been one of the main causes of my illness. Which was the real me, and which was the façade? That was a question I often asked myself. In truth, both were part of who I was, but it was a hard act to balance.

Anyway, through research I discovered the simple fact that most of the chicken sold in the UK as halal is actually haram. Haram is the opposite of halal: it means that the bird or animal is dead before the incision is made. It contravenes Muslim faith to eat haram, and I'd spent hours arguing with the Muslim Council of Britain that their silence was betraying their community. But I guess money talks louder. If any other consumer group was being conned like this there'd be a public outcry. Big fast-food outlets were claiming to sell halal chicken with little or no understanding of what that meant. Just driven by the dollar.

It was because of these efforts that Saracen was nominated for, and received, a global award for innovation in the halal industry. We had designed a mechanical system to calm the birds and reduce damage from the killing process. I had to travel to Kuala Lumpur for the prize-giving ceremony, accompanied by my friend, Youssef Pandor.

Youssef is a devout Muslim and one of the funniest and most charismatic people I've ever met. His commitment to his principles and his community are impressive. He only ever eats halal food, and sticks to fish unless he trusts the halal certification of a venue, where he'll order chicken. He never uses cutlery, and instead uses his naan to move the food from the plate to his mouth. No matter what size the meal, he always has a tiny piece of bread left to clean his plate.

We were staying in a decent hotel within shouting distance of the famous Petronas towers, and it struck me as strange to see such displays of wealth while so many destitute locals moved through the streets below. It had been the same in Thailand, the disparity between the rich and the poor, so much more obvious and on display.

The presentation concluded the three-day seminar. It was a proud moment when we took to the stage and received applause for our hard work. And although the travel was amazing, all I could think about, while I was away, was Rhoda and the time we'd spent together since that night in Norwich. We'd seen each other almost every weekend, with either me going down to Norwich or her visiting Hope Valley. I knew my feelings for her were growing, and I'd made it plain that I wanted her to move up to Castleton to live with me.

Within walking distance of our Kuala Lumpur hotel, a large market sold tat to tourists. And I joined in wholeheartedly. Keeping Rhoda in my thoughts, I bought numerous fake designer handbags and other items. As long as it was emblazoned with a Chanel or Gucci label it would go down a storm with her. I filled my luggage with cheap watches, jewellery and bags. And she loved every item. Was I consciously courting her to move up and live with me? I wasn't aware of it at the time, but I was putting in all that effort with the house in Derbyshire to tempt her up there to live.

The house was coming along nicely. From the start my approach was to get things right from the beginning, as this was my forever home. I recruited some rugby mates to help out with the plastering and electrical work as this was beyond my skill set. When the building work had started I'd moved into a pub up the road, striking a good deal for a long-term let on a room. But that was all costing money so I hurried to move in as fast as possible. I ripped out the old bathroom and converted it into a wet room, and most of the place had new ceilings and freshly plastered walls.

Rhoda hated the colours I'd chosen, and that was fair enough. They were fairly dark and dull, typical shades picked by a guy living on his own. The one room she loved was the converted third bedroom. I'd railed it out as a walk-in wardrobe with a top shelf all the way round for shoes and boots. There was a dressing-table and a mirror, and it became her favourite room in the house. Over a few weekends we'd moved in loads of her clothes and personal stuff. Tony had put the furniture she didn't want into storage, and we planned one last trip with him using his Luton-body truck. Just three days before the final haul Rhoda mentioned her dogs.

'Dogs?'

'Yes, my Chihuahuas.'

'How many are there?' She'd probably mentioned them, but I'd obviously forgotten they even existed.

'Twelve at the moment.'

'Twelve.'

'But the last two bitches are pregnant, so there'll be more within a few weeks.'

Jesus. A dozen and counting. Rhoda had bred Chihuahuas for a while but we'd hardly talked about it. She knew I liked dogs, and that my Alfie was a pet and my constant companion. Those rat-like animals weren't pets as I knew them, more a source of income.

'So what do I need to build?' I asked. 'Whelping pens?' I could hear the dread in my voice.

Rhoda said we'd get away with three pens and described what was needed. After finding some sheet timber I set about constructing a row of hutches for the imminent arrival of a Chihuahua herd.

We carried them in, tiny dogs with even tinier off-spring. The bitches had names like Tinkerbell, Chanel and Vogue. Alfie looked baffled. What were these new creatures that now shared his home?

The Chihuahua army soon bunkered in. Well, until the night we discovered Tinkerbell had escaped from the back garden. It was late summer so we had plenty of light and launched a search party.

'Tinkerbell! Tinkerbell!' Rhoda was calling loudly. 'Well, join in!' she shouted at me.

'Tinks,' I mumbled. 'Tinker!' I said half-heartedly. I had little enthusiasm to wander around my new village shouting, 'Tinkerbell,' at the top of my voice. But that's exactly what happened, and after a very embarrassing hour the dog was found across some meadows.

The dogs didn't come into the house much, but once the garden was secure they'd play out there endlessly. You'd have to be made of stone not to find a dozen or more puppies entertaining. Alfie was already a big dog, yet he was gentle enough to let the youngest scamps hang on to his legs with their sharp teeth. When they got to eight weeks they started disappearing to their own forever homes, and the Chihuahua population dropped off in the household.

Once Rhoda started unpacking her belongings I saw just how obsessed with Disney she was. Dozens and dozens of intricate and valuable water globes showing scenes from the various movies were stacked everywhere. A couple had been put out on display but I'd stood my ground and kept the majority in boxes. We often had a massive difference of opinion on decor. I was more for the traditional country style, mixed with a few items brought back from my travels. Rhoda was all pink and diamanté, and everything had to be branded, from cushions, crockery and mirrors to the loo brush.

Interior-design differences aside, our first weeks were amazing. I was now firm friends with the family who owned the Cheshire Cheese, and Rhoda quickly became friends with the daughters who helped run it. Every night we wandered up and round the pubs, free from our dog-minding duties now we were down to just a couple of Chihuahuas: Rhoda had sold most of them and rehomed the breeding bitches with her extended family in Essex.

My work was going well – the business seemed to be booming, judging by Sam's weekly reports. I was getting more and more involved with Hope Valley Rugby Club, helping to coach and recruit players as well as organize social nights. Rhoda loved those events: local night life was quiet compared to what she was used to. At the lively rugby socials she came into her own. We had a Smurf-themed night where everyone was blue, apart from Steve, one of our younger players. He hadn't been able to get any blue face paint so he'd coloured himself all over with a green felt tip. Hilarious. When snow blanketed the village we arranged a fox-and-hounds evening, where all the girlfriends and ladies from the villages dressed up as foxes, and the lads as huntsmen. Drinking along a set route, the foxes had a one-hour head start then the huntsmen would follow. Foxes were allowed shorts and shots, and the hounds had to sink a pint in each venue. It was glorious chaos, with both groups ending up at a disco.

These were some of my happiest times for years. I had my new home, Rhoda on my arm, Alfie, Saracen was doing well, and I was loving my rugby in the valley. I couldn't see what could go wrong.

20

I'd made my mind up that my future lay in Derbyshire. All the troubles I'd had with the Travellers now seemed a distant memory. Months had gently rolled into years since the fights and the burnings, and life in the Peak District was such a contrast, although farmers in the valley reported lots of thefts, with quad bikes and red diesel constantly going missing. Both Sheffield and Manchester had large Traveller communities, and the Peak District offered easy pickings in a rural landscape with no real police presence, once again. But it wasn't a personal issue for me any more. I was done with that and just wanted to focus on my new life.

Living with Rhoda had also brought me into contact with Gypsy culture in new ways. She often talked of her grandparents, famous Essex Romany folk, with a proud heritage and sense of tradition. There were books on Gypsy history that detailed generations of her family. Grainy black-and-white photos of swarthy men and dark-haired women sitting at the front of their vardos, the classic Gypsy wagons. The vardos would contain an entire family and their possessions, and if there were too many folk for the wagon some of the family might sleep underneath it. Wood-fired cooking ranges were skilfully built into the larger wagons, and the smoke stack poked through an insulated hole in the canvas.

Rhoda told me that the colours and flowers painted on them denoted the family and their lineage: they weren't just for decoration. Other families would recognize the images and acknowledge and respect the history involved.

I imagined living in one of those wagons, editing my life down to such a simple format, carrying only what was vital for survival, nothing frivolous or unnecessary. The only items that were commonly held to show wealth or for decoration were Crown Derby china. The intricate red, blue and gold porcelain motifs appealed to Gypsy folk and most had at least a few items on display. Rhoda had some bits and pieces, and I knew her father, Tony, had an extensive collection.

Rhoda also talked about the importance of horses in traditional Gypsy culture, the care and attention devoted to their breeding. Without good horse stock you were stuck, unable to move on to the next harvest, the next seasonal work. Most Gypsies take a lot of pride in breeding and showing the quality of their horses. Listening to Rhoda, I could tell that it had been a hard life for her grandparents and the generations before them, a community that had lived in caravans and trailers. Now that they had moved into motor vehicles the horses were more symbolic than a vital method of transport. Rhoda's mother was one of six girls, raised on the move to suit wherever her grandparents could find work. But they also had no mortgage, no taxes to pay, and no bureaucratic authority looming over them, dictating their daily life, like the rest of society.

I liked the sound of this: a wonderful freedom from the trappings of everyday living. I started to research some of the culture that Rhoda spoke of and it made interesting reading. The true history of the Romany is clouded in mystery and subject to many theories, but their origins lay on the other side of the Mediterranean Sea, as far round as what was then Persia, and now Iran. Looking at Rhoda, as I often did, it was clear to see those features in her bloodline. The dark eyes, the cheekbones, the long black hair. She was beautiful and exotic.

The more I learnt, the more I regretted my actions back in Norfolk.

I'd been in touch with Will and Jason, who had heard no ongoing threats to track us down. Some good friends in Ledburgh had repeated comments made in the pubs down there about my moving away, and maybe a few folk had their suspicions, but that was all. I felt as though I'd put all of that firmly behind me.

Rhoda moving in had changed my world. Again. We spent our time sorting out the house and socializing. She was an instant hit with the locals. The lads couldn't believe she was with me, and the girls loved her. She had a very open, warm character, which gained her lots of close friends. For me this was a relief. I'd moved up there with an established social life from years of holidays, but this was all new to Rhoda, yet she fitted right into the community.

One of my biggest concerns about her moving up was the lack of a metropolitan social life. I'd always seen her out enjoying herself in bars and restaurants, or shopping in town centres. Life there was vastly different. But the girls of the valley adored her from the start. We held dinner parties, ladies-only affairs, where I did the cooking and serving, then cleared off to the pub, leaving the sound of laughter echoing behind me in the lanes. Those evenings were a great success, and Rhoda's tales of nights at the Sugar Hut, meeting celebrities and mixing with the *TOWIE* crowd there were such a contrast with time spent among the rural valley girls. Rhoda seemed happy and settled, and it was time to focus on the future.

I'd come up to Derbyshire with enough funds and income to live for a while, but they wouldn't last for ever. I had plans to hand over Saracen, so my income from the business had to be replaced at some point. Rhoda was all about glamour, a classic Essex girl: everything had to be just right, hair, suntan, make-up, nails, clothes and shoes. We sat and talked about what we could do.

'I've got some money. Maybe we could get a pub,' I suggested.

'I'm not living in a pub,' she quickly replied. 'It never ends well.'

She was right. It was very rare that couples lasted as publicans.

'How about a nice shop?' she wondered.

'Selling what?' The only successful shops in the valley sold walking and climbing gear, and that market was already crowded. 'What do you really know about?' I asked her. 'What are you really good at?'

Rhoda hadn't had any sort of formal career, and her father had taken her out of school at twelve years old, once she'd mastered basic reading, writing and arithmetic. It was the Gypsy way. They couldn't understand why their children should learn about fourteenth-century crop rotation or how to speak German. They could be out earning a pound, helping the family turn a profit. There was also the issue of mixing with boys at a vulnerable age. Gypsy girls are fiercely protected by the men of the family: fathers, uncles and brothers are strict guardians of a young girl's honour. Modern sex education and young adolescents getting carried away had been more than Tony could take.

Rhoda had left school without a single certificate to her name, so her employment history was a bit random. Although her lack of a general education sometimes showed in our chosen topics of conversation, it was never a hindrance to her getting on in life. She had the natural intelligence to achieve anything she wanted, but lacked interest in subjects she'd never been encouraged to explore, or had simply left school before studying. Regardless, she was a savvy young woman who used her most obvious powers to full effect.

'I'm good at looking good.'

It was a flippant, cheerful remark, but oh-so-true.

'Yes, you are,' I said, and kissed her.

And what had been a throwaway comment began a serious conversation. She had the people skills and understanding to open and run a beauty salon. Combined with my head for business, it might work. After lots of planning and talking things through, we decided to open not just a salon but a venue that would provide everything. Rhoda could be front of house and I could do the business end of the project. We agreed to call it Heaven.

I found a venue in Hope, the next village. An old bank was going to be available at the end of the month. In return for an extensive refurbishment, for which we would be responsible, we shook hands with the owners on a three-month rent-free period and signed the lease. It was a hectic but happy time. Rhoda was sourcing equipment and stock, and I was cracking on with the building work.

'I've found a street in Manchester where they sell bags and shoes wholesale,' Rhoda said excitedly. 'We can go and have a look, see what's available.'

Within two months we'd bought sunbeds, a huge spray-tan booth, everything for a three-chair hair salon, a nail bar, white leather massage bed, and enough high-heeled shoes and handbags to fill a football stadium. Rhoda had always wanted to sell clothes, too, so I added a room full of rails. All of the stock was top-end, the clothes Forever Unique, a label favoured by the *TOWIE* girls.

The sunbeds needed a heavy-duty electrical cable to power them up and fry the locals, so we had to take up some floorboards to lay in a supply through the building. During the excavation we came across something from a horror film. To our shock we found the top of a human skull and some bony fingers poking out of the soil below the floor. What the hell had happened here? The building was opposite the village church, but it was a long way for a corpse to burrow under the road, so we called the local police. They drove out and calmly explained that in the local area it had been a tradition to bury a cadaver in the foundations of any pub or inn, and the building had started life as a coaching inn hundreds of years ago. The police simply covered the bones with earth and placed a laminated sign over the top explaining what was buried below. I laughed with friends that if you ever wanted to get away with murder just bury the body under the foundations of a Derbyshire pub.

Before we'd even opened the doors I'd invested more than a hundred thousand pounds. But the results were amazing. Folk in the area had never seen anything like it in the valley. Pure Essex bling, pink walls, and diamanté glittering everywhere you looked. Rhoda was ecstatic.

We planned a grand opening party, inviting everyone we knew and many we didn't. Boxes and boxes of champagne, posh nibbles and a red carpet. On the big night it looked more like a nightclub opening than a hair and beauty salon. All the guests had dressed up in their finest, and it was packed. Crowds gathered outside, laughing and chatting, enjoying the occasion. It was incredible. Total success. Rhoda was wearing one of the Forever

Unique dresses and looked better than ever. We were taking bookings for all of the different parts of the salon, while curious locals and friends were looking round the venue and complimenting us on our hard work. It did look amazing. I felt so proud of what we had achieved, and as I watched Rhoda chatting with people who were becoming her clients, I was proud of her, too.

This was the future, our bright new beginning. With dark shadows looming.

21

I was busy getting the shop going when I took an odd phone call from Sam, back at Saracen. It was only then that I recalled he hadn't been at the opening for Heaven.

'How are things going, Sam?' I asked, interested in the yard but also keen to tell him about the successful launch party.

'Could be better, if I'm honest,' he replied.

There was a tone in his voice I hadn't heard before. Over the years we'd become good friends and he'd always been grateful for my help. Not to mention I'd been best man at his wedding the summer before. I knew something was wrong just from the way he spoke to me on the phone.

'Can you come to the office on Friday?'

I said of course, and the call was ended with no discussion of my good news. The uneasy feeling in my gut soon passed, as we were still celebrating the opening night and the initial success of the salon. There'd been a continuous stream of ladies booking in for hair and nail treatments, and the upright sunbeds were a big hit, with customers buying twenty-quid sessions to stand in a booth and get blasted by UV rays for three minutes at a time. Rhoda was beyond happy. She was surrounded by expensive clothes, shoes and bags, and lapping up the popularity and attention that came with owning the venue.

Anyway, I drove to Norfolk for my meeting with Sam. I arrived in the yard and did my usual round of greetings with the lads. I'd interviewed and employed most of them. We'd worked long hours together, and had bonded on various engineering projects. But something was wrong, I could feel it. This was confirmed when I walked into the office and found Sam and Colin, the managers, sitting with a third man I'd never laid eyes on before.

'All right, Sam. Who's this?'

Sitting beside him was a typical suit. By that I mean a guy who has worn a shirt and tie every working day of his life since he started high school. Fastidiously clean, crisply ironed lines on his trousers. A fine pinstripe that was a compromise between fashion and what a banker would wear. Alert eyes met my gaze from a poker face. Hands so clean I wondered who wiped his arse.

The man stood up, shook my hand and introduced himself. And that was the end of all the niceties.

'I'm an insolvency agent, and as of today your business is insolvent and it will be illegal to trade.'

My universe lurched to the side. I turned to Sam and Colin. Neither of them would look me in the eye. I felt sick. How had this happened? We had a solid customer base, a great team and a great product.

'What's happened, Sam?' I asked, my voice full of disbelief.

'It's cash flow,' he mumbled. 'We've just been quiet.'

I turned to the insolvency agent. He explained again that, now I'd been informed of the situation, it was illegal for me to trade. At all. Meaning there was no way I could raise funds to buy some time. It was over.

There was something very wrong here. I sensed it in the air. I took the paperwork he handed me, politely told him to fuck off out of my office, and sat down with my head in my hands. Sam started to make small-talk, as though what had just happened didn't matter. The sense of shock I was feeling said differently. I had a friend in the valley who'd been doing the accounts, and I trusted him. I needed to see him urgently. I called the lads off the tools and into the canteen.

'It looks like the firm is in a spot of bother,' I explained. Understatement of the year. 'I'm going back up to the valley to try and sort things out.'

I made a promise to the lads that I'd do everything in my power to keep things going. I was watching their faces. Sam and Colin were staring at the floor, looking guilty as hell. And there were plenty of hard stares from the other lads going in their direction, too. Although the penny still hadn't dropped as to what had actually gone down there.

I got into the car and floored it back to Hope Valley, heading straight to my accountant. He confirmed what the insolvency officer had said, and that in terms of cash flow, yes, Saracen was insolvent. Had we been allowed to juggle a bit we could have worked through it.

The problem was that no new work had been taken on in the last three months, which meant no deposits for future projects. For the first time I began to suspect something had been planned. So we did a quick search on Companies House, and there it was in black and white. Sam and Colin had registered a business in their own names a few months before. I kept reading the dates. I'd spent time with both of them after the registration. We'd laughed together, been out for drinks. What sort of low-life bastards would do this? I'd promised them that I would hand over the business in time, but greed and impatience had forced them to pull the trigger early.

I felt that they'd struck a deal with this insolvency firm so I appointed another. And that turned out just as badly. Saracen closed on a Friday, and Steyn, the new company owned by Sam and Colin, opened a week later. In my office, in my chair, using my equipment, vehicles and tools. Some of my old staff and all of my customers. I heard later that they boasted about taking hundreds of thousands of pounds in orders in their first two weeks of trading. All the missing orders from Saracen's last three months. They'd got away with it. Two guys I'd considered my best friends had plotted and schemed to remove me from the business I'd started from nothing.

The urge to drive down to the yard with a chainsaw was overwhelming. But I had to restrain my emotions. I had a new life now and I had to focus on that. I also had my medical history to consider. The aneurysm had been stress-related. I knew they'd taken advantage of my illness to make their plans, and that hurt most. I swore an oath never to forget what they'd done but not to react immediately. I must be patient: our paths will cross again, when I'm ready and prepared to have my justice.

22

That was a terrible time. My mind was all over the place after Sam and Colin betrayed me. As the weeks went by, more information came out about how devious they'd been. It made me feel sick if I dwelt on what had happened, and the process had left me in serious debt. Legally I had to find fifty grand to pay the insolvency agent after the sale of my business. It hurt to think that while I was struggling they were enjoying such success.

All this had a serious effect on Rhoda. There was no spare cash to keep the salon stocked with new designs. Things got tighter and tighter. I sat down and really studied the books from the salon. We were losing money. Badly. The initial interest in the glitzy enterprise had faded. I had thousands and thousands of pounds' worth of stock just sitting there. Bookings in the hair salon had crashed, and I was losing about four hundred pounds a week. Had been for months. How had I missed it?

I sat down with Rhoda. We needed to go through the figures in a very basic and realistic way.

'I'm running out of money,' I said, stating the obvious. 'At this rate we've got about two months left before we get into a real muddle.'

'Is it that serious?' Rhoda almost whispered. I could

hear the pain in her voice. The salon had been her dream. But I was about to drop an even bigger bombshell. We weren't going to lose only the salon: we might lose the house as well.

That was the first big thing we had to deal with as a couple. Until then everything had been easy; romance, the new home, the salon. We'd been having fun running around spending thousands of pounds. Feeling invincible. This would be a real test of how strong we were together.

Within a week it had happened. My only option was to sell my home, my beloved cottage in Castleton. The equity from the house would just about cover the debts and leave a few grand to start again somewhere else. Rhoda was devastated. There was little I could say to make her feel better. I think I felt worse.

We put the salon up for sale as a going concern and retained the stock of clothes, shoes and handbags. Luckily I managed to find a buyer who lived locally and was keen to give it a go. I clawed back a few grand from the sale, but the truth was I'd have let the business go for a fiver. The deal was done, and the new owners were re-designing the place before we'd even closed the door behind us. They wanted a change of style more in keeping with the country folk of the valley, which, of course, made complete sense. Oh, for the power of hindsight.

So the shop was gone. Now for the house. But we needed somewhere to live.

'I'm stuck for an answer, darling.'

And it was true. I genuinely had no idea what to think or do. The equity from the house was legally promised to the Saracen liquidators. One of the first things they'd done was to force the sale and lay claim to any equity from our home. We might have eked out some funds from the sale of the salon, but there wasn't much. We'd be lucky to get out of the situation broke but debt-free.

'I can have a word with Dad,' offered Rhoda.

'I don't want us borrowing money,' I replied. 'I'm owing enough in every direction as it is.'

'That's not what I'm saying. He has a plot of land near Colchester. We might be able to go down there, make a new start.'

The valley had lost its appeal for her. The shame of losing the salon and our home wasn't something that sat well with her Gypsy pride. Combined with that, I sensed she was content simply to move on. To relocate and start again. Most women would have been devastated, but not Rhoda. For her being on the move was fine, an accepted part of Gypsy life. So the call was made and Tony came to our rescue.

He'd bought a plot of land near Colchester as a young man. It had sat untouched for forty years, and was now ours to live on if we wanted. Tony had always been straight with me and I knew this was a genuine offer. We certainly needed the help.

Still, I couldn't get my head round us living in a caravan on Gypsy land, relying on the goodwill of Tony for a home. The only way my mind would accept it was that this was the first step to building a house: we'd get planning permission to start a project, our own home, and begin the journey back to normality.

My sense of normality. My family had nice houses, modern cars and mortgages, good careers. They were part of the local community. They were teachers, dentists and builders. I was now way past the black-sheep status. Moving into a caravan on Gypsy land wasn't something I could face talking about to any member of my family and I was feeling more and more isolated. On Facebook I put on a brave front of a new beginning, a chance to build my own home. But inside I was devastated. This move symbolized everything I'd lost. My home, my businesses, the Range Rover. My whole life had vanished before my eyes.

For Rhoda it was different. This land had been earmarked for her as an inheritance sometime in the future. The area was surrounded by her family, aunts and uncles, cousins and grandparents. I was feeling ever more isolated from my gorgia roots, family and friends. I was rapidly being absorbed into Rhoda's Romany world.

I went down to look at the plot and meet Tony. It was in Elmstead Market, a village just outside Colchester. I pulled up behind Tony's car and got out to a warm handshake.

'Morning, Tony,' I said. 'How are you?'

'Getting by. How's Rhoda?' Tony's first question was always after his daughter and how she was. He was a good father.

'Where's this plot, then, Tony?'

'It's here,' he replied, waving his arm to the side, towards a dense jungle of the thickest brambles and blackthorn trees I'd ever seen. 'I haven't been down here for a while, and haven't touched the place since I bought it.'

It showed. Forty years of untamed growth. Hawthorn, blackthorn and brambles offered a seemingly impenetrable frontage. But we pushed in through the bushes and Tony showed me the extent of the plot. It was huge. The boundaries had never been fenced in, and I realized the only reason it hadn't become a local tipping ground was its inaccessibility from the road. It was ideal for us to build a home on. I thanked Tony and headed back up the M1 to Rhoda, keen to tell her some good news at last.

The house had been on the market for a couple of weeks. Properties sold fast in Castleton, which was a popular tourist village, and holiday homes were a good investment.

Sam and Colin's actions had not only taken my business and forced me to sell my home, but it looked as though I'd lose most of the equity as well. We'd be heading down to Essex with little more than the clothes on our backs. I needed to get my act together and make preparations on the new plot to make it liveable.

23

Up went the For Sale sign on my lovely home. It was a horrible feeling, seeing it there, advertising to the world our downfall. We'd gone from having a gorgeous cottage in a wonderful village, owning the salon and living the dream, to this, a public spectacle of failure. I felt like tearing it down and throwing it into the river. But we needed to sell the house, so the sign remained, even though every time I saw it my guts twisted.

Within days a friend, and I now use that word loosely, came to see us about buying it. She'd lived in a rented property in the village for years since her separation from her husband, and wanted to stay close to him for her children's sake. We talked it through and I touched on the reason I couldn't drop any more off the price. She started crying, explaining that she really needed to stay in the area. 'This is the perfect house,' she sobbed, 'but I can only afford so much.'

I talked it through with Rhoda: accepting this low offer would leave us with very little to restart our lives in Essex. But the would-be buyer was a friend and she was desperate. So we shook hands and the house was sold.

I later found out that within weeks of moving in she'd blown forty grand on refurbishing the property. I'd been royally hoodwinked. Maybe if things hadn't been so desperate for us I'd have seen through her patter. It still leaves a bitter taste in my mouth whenever I remember those crocodile tears.

After the deal was done on the house we had about six weeks before the legal completion date when we had to leave. Over the next month I regularly travelled down to Elmstead Market to work on clearing the plot and get things ready for the move. Tony's friend, Joe, another Traveller from near Ledburgh, had a three-tonne 360 digger, which would make light work of clearing the undergrowth. The plan was for me to travel down and stay with Rhoda's cousin while I was clearing the land for a caravan. Yes, a caravan. Similar to the kind I'd once lobbed petrol bombs at in the dead of night. A caravan I was yet to buy with money I didn't have. That depended on securing a sale of the salon lease and equipment.

Curious, and no doubt nervous, as to what lifestyle awaited her, Rhoda drove down with me to see the plot. She also came along to introduce me to Eddie and his wife, Sara, another of her cousins. Eddie, like me, was a gorgia with a Romany partner.

On the way to Eddie's home we called at the plot so Rhoda could see the task ahead.

'Oh, my God!' she exclaimed, as soon I pulled on to the untamed land. 'It's like a jungle.' She stared at the thick bushes and trees that enveloped the site.

'It's hard to picture it now,' I tried to comfort her, 'but most of this will be gone in a couple of days.' I was trying to sound upbeat, and failing miserably. 'We'll be okay,' I said, putting my arms around her.

We left the plot in a sombre mood, and headed for her cousin's home a couple of miles away.

Eddie and Sara had readily offered to put me up while I did the work on the land. I was made welcome, treated as family right from the start. It was comforting to have a friend in the area. Eddie was larger than life, juggling various building jobs, keeping everyone happy enough but always lining up the next bit of work. His main contract was on the docks at Felixstowe and he said I could do some days for him to get some income. Things were looking more positive, and maybe there was light at the end of the tunnel. It never crossed my mind that I was becoming more and more involved in the Travelling community.

It became obvious as time for the move drew closer that all of the people helping me were Travellers. As I sat on the land designing the basic layout, everybody involved in my plans was either a Gypsy or connected to them. And that help was willingly offered, without hesitation. Nothing was too much trouble, and everyone was glad to lend a hand. My face burnt with the shame of my previous attitude, and actions, towards these hard-working and big-hearted folk.

Over the next month, with the added muscle of my new community, I cleared the land. Joe, a Traveller friend of Tony's, met me on the site with his digger and made short work of ripping down trees and scraping out all the brambles. Eddie was there, fag in his mouth, felling the larger trees with a chainsaw. Once we'd cleared a way on to the plot I bought some large wooden gates and posts. Everybody was saying to get the plot secure, make sure nobody could just pull on into it. I could always burn them out, I thought grimly, but kept those memories to myself.

I laid some concrete pads, one for a trailer and one for my garden shed, which was still in Derbyshire. I took delivery of a 40-foot shipping container to use as secure storage. The gates were hung, chains and padlocks put in place. It was taking shape nicely.

Rhoda and I had decided to buy a large static trailer to live in, then start saving to build a house. We went to a dealer in Thorrington, just down the road, and shook hands on a three-grand unit, which would be delivered at the end of the week. It was a bit rough on the outside but tidy enough within. And it was all I could afford. I was spending a fraction on our home of what some friends were spending on a car. It was a sobering thought.

When the trailer turned up on the back of a lorry it looked huge. Well, it was to be our home. The lads towed it in from the road using a Land Rover and started positioning it on the concrete pad.

'There's a couple of men at the gate,' one of the lads said, pointing under the caravan. I'd shut the gates as I had Alfie with me and didn't want him running on to the road.

Sure enough, two guys were standing by the gates. They looked harmless enough so I wandered over.

'Can I help you?' I asked.

'We're from the council,' informed the older man. 'Here to serve an enforcement order.'

'On who? What about?'

'On the occupier of this land. Once the notice is served you can't pull any caravans on this site.'

'Once the notice is served,' I repeated. 'This one's already on here.'

'I know,' he replied. 'If we hadn't stopped for a cup of tea on the way here you wouldn't have been able to pull that one on.'

The notice gave warning of a hefty fine if any caravans were parked after that date and time. I'd been minutes from disaster. Had the notice gone up before we'd got the trailer off the road, I'd have lost most of my money and had nowhere to call my home. I chatted with the council guys. They were decent enough blokes, just doing their job. The local authority had been through a nightmare near the village with a group of Travellers setting up camp and causing trouble. They didn't want the same thing to happen here. I felt judged, suddenly on the other side of the argument about Travellers, but mainly I was relieved we'd got the trailer on to the plot. Now we had somewhere to sleep, and plenty of storage space for all of the things from the house.

It was a hell of a fall from grace, and once again my dark thoughts about Sam and Colin returned.

24

We still had a few weeks left in the house in Hope Valley. We were busy packing our life into boxes, and it was feeling very real that we were leaving. Rhoda had made some really good friends, and I could see how upset she was. To try to take the edge off things, we organized a few nights out with different groups of friends, some lovely people we'd got to know in our time in the community. They were special evenings, farewell dinners and drinks, but saying goodbye at the end of the night was awful, and it got worse each time. But I had to put a brave face on things. We both did.

Apart from all our personal possessions, we still had loads of shoes and bags from the salon to sell. We desperately needed to turn our dead stock into ready cash, and I'd already been to a few county fairs and flogged our wares with some success. I'd driven up to Newcastle to buy a second-hand marquee, and booked a spot at half a dozen such events – I'd scoured the internet for places to set up a stall and make some money. The main hurdle was the fees, which could be as high as five hundred pounds for a six-metre frontage, meaning the first thousand pounds of sales would just cover costs.

After working a few of the more professionally run

events I soon had an idea of which ones were the better earners. Some were a right rip-off for the public, charging top dollar to walk around a glorified market. Families had already spent up to a hundred pounds on entrance, food and drink, so were unlikely to be buying handbags. The best weekends were the steam rallies or vintage-car shows, any day out where there was a genuine draw. Pitches were cheaper, and the folk wandering round seemed happier. It was a risk, but my enthusiastic sales methods paid off. I'd spot a lady wearing a blue scarf with pink spots, grab a handbag that matched, and chase after her offering a discount. It was hard work on my own, setting up the stand and being on my feet all day, but I was slowly turning the stock back into cash. And, by Christ, we needed it.

What made it possible was the camaraderie of the other stallholders. There was a real sense of solidarity and genuine offers of help between us all. I soon became aware that most of the traders had a Travelling background. They were either Gypsy heritage, or somehow related. And they were good people. Hard workers, grafting long hours, but ready to offer a hand or some advice. They used to open the beer tent at night for the traders and it was always a good laugh. Beer flowed and cash was spent.

I enjoyed those weekends but I often found myself feeling confused and uncomfortable. Sitting around drinking and telling stories, the traders would often talk of the injustices they'd faced over the years, the endless arguments and disputes with local councils, police forces and groups of upstanding community members, none of whom seemed able to accept their way of life. I sat quiet through these discussions. I could feel my cheeks burning with shame on hearing a story where a family had lost their home after a farmer had tipped a caravan over with a JCB.

These were people I could be friends with. They were more willing than my own community to lend a hand, offer food or drink to a stranger. And the more time I was spending with them the more regret I felt at my level of ignorance in the past. Not towards the Smiths, they were just arseholes, regardless of any claim of Travelling heritage. But towards the genuine Travellers, moving around and trying to make a living wherever they could. Fighting against massive odds, and losing nearly every time.

Rhoda suggested going to sell the handbags at Stow Horse Fair, one of the largest gatherings of Travelling folk in the country. As Rhoda had selected the bags in the first place, she knew they'd appeal to the Gypsy community.

The horse fair at Stow has its roots in the Norman Conquest expansion of European trade nearly a thousand years ago. Once the wool business slowed in the area, and shepherds no longer drove flocks of sheep through Stow's narrow alleys to be sold, what had been a market gradually transformed into the horse fair it is today, offering a chance for all those Travellers unable to go to Appleby Horse Fair in Cumbria to get together. As Stow sits at the meeting point of eight ancient trackways, traders and way-farers from across the country often passed through the

Cotswolds town throughout its long history on the journey to sell their goods. Everything from silk to salt to fish and iron, along with the products of traditional craft work, such as weaving, pottery and spinning, has been bought and bartered there over the centuries, and now I was about to set up a stall flogging shoes and handbags.

'I've got a contact number for you to call,' Rhoda told me. 'Just say you're friends with Riley and Tillie. You'll be okay.'

Riley and Tillie were Rhoda's grandparents, well known in the Gypsy world, and arrangements were quickly made. After all that had happened all those years ago, I was actually going to trade at a traditional Gypsy horse fair.

I was nervous about going down on my own so I took a friend from Sheffield with me. Andy was a brick shithouse of a doorman who'd just started playing rugby with the Hope Valley team. We'd enjoyed a few evenings sampling beers together, and had become good friends.

We decided to drive down the night before to secure a decent pitch and get set up.

Andy got into the van, filling the passenger seat. 'So what's the score, then?'

'Easy enough,' I said, trying to sound confident. 'We just set all the stuff out, crash in the tent tonight, and sell what we can tomorrow.'

It was a one-day event, and no matter how late we finished, the plan was to break down the stall and head home that night.

After the long drive we arrived at the site and drove through a gap in the hedge. A cluster of men was standing around the bonnet of a white van, so I parked and wandered over to them. This was an odd moment for me. Somehow I felt almost drunk, and my brain couldn't focus. These men could easily be connected to those Traveller families from years before and I was about to shake their hands and immerse myself fully in their world. It was obvious from my van and trailer that I was there to trade. Would I be made welcome?

'Can I help you, young fella?' asked an older chap sitting in a van.

I extended my palm to feel a warm handshake. Large hands worn soft by a lifetime of graft. 'I called last week. I'm with Riley and Tillie's granddaughter.'

They all looked at my van, seeing the bulk of Andy just sitting there.

'Oh, she's not here,' I added. 'I've come down to sell some bags.' I felt more of an outsider by the second.

'I know Riley,' said the old chap. 'A good man, a good man.'

The atmosphere changed immediately. It was then I understood how important family and family names were to the Gypsy community. Simply through a tenuous connection we'd been made welcome.

One of the younger Gypsy lads took us round the field and showed us where to set up. I was happy enough with the location, and Andy and I got stuck into readying the stall.

We finished arranging the bags as other traders arrived. They continued to turn up throughout the night, the glow of headlights beaming across the field and lighting up my marquee. The clatter of steel bars and the quiet exchange of greetings went on during the hours of darkness as the stalls were erected. Andy and I shared a few beers before crashing out on roll mats in our sleeping bags.

We got some sleep and woke early to a sunny day. Except the field was a mud bath, despite the sunshine. Recent rain and the many vans and trucks had made a mess of the main routes around the fair. Folk were still coming in to set up though, and all were telling stories about how the police had erected a cordon around the area to check everyone's goods with a trading-standards officer. They were searching for dodgy gear and fake brands, which was almost everything that was being sold.

I swear every item on sale was emblazoned with a well-known brand, from bathroom rugs to baby clothes, all with Chanel or Gucci logos plastered over them. Usually pink and covered in diamanté. The police had confiscated the goods and vehicles of at least thirty traders, leaving them on the roadside to walk the rest of the way in. Tempers were already high, and listening to the stories, I sympathized with the traders. Why couldn't the police leave them alone? The fake goods were so obviously fake they'd only be bought by other Travellers. So what if they wanted a pair of leopard-print wellies with a Gucci logo on the side?

And the heavy-handed manner was way over the top. Taking vehicles and stranding women and children on the roadside was wrong. The relationship between those families and the police would never recover.

A more traditional part of the gathering is horse-trading. Meadows filled with Gypsy ponies surrounded the fair, along with groups of men talking hard and shaking hands on sales. Flying overhead, a police helicopter was filming the event, which meant hovering low. This upset the horses, causing numerous escapes and galloping runaways chased by anxious owners. It was plain to see that the police knew exactly what they were doing, and how it was affecting the horses. But it seemed more important to upset the Gypsy fair than show any concern for animal welfare.

Despite the authorities' spoiling tactics, the fair went ahead on time, dozens of stalls selling everything from handmade leather boots to crystal-encrusted oven gloves. Both Andy and I took a turn to wander round and have a look before the crowds arrived. It wasn't long before people were turning up in serious numbers. There was another meadow for public car parking and it was a sight to behold. The high-end cars rolling into that meadow were unbelievable – Mercedes, Range Rovers, BMWs, Bentleys and Porsches, all brand new, highly polished, and not one more than six months old.

'Fuck me!' I exclaimed. 'Look at that lot, Andy.' I pointed at the car park. 'There's some serious coin over there.'

'How do they afford cars like that?' Andy asked me.

'They don't own them,' explained the lady next to us. She was from Southend, selling baby clothes, all with Chanel and Versace labels on. She'd followed us in the night before and slipped through the cordon with her fake merchandise. 'They hire them for the day to turn up and show off.' She laughed. 'Those cars will be wrecked by tonight.'

She seemed friendly enough, so I decided to ask her about the fake baby gear. 'Don't get me wrong, but if your gear's all logoed up with fake brands, don't you worry about them coming round and taking it away?'

'You cheeky beggar!' She laughed again. 'How do you know they're fake?'

'Well . . .' I shrugged, grinning.

'Look, once you're in, then you're in.' She started laying out her table in Gucci tea towels. 'And if the police came on the field there would be a riot, so they pick us off on the road, when we're on our own, and leave us alone if we're in big enough numbers.'

Like bullies, I thought. Only picking on the weak. It made perfect sense, and explained why she'd driven in the night before. And it was well worth her efforts, as she did a roaring trade all day. It seemed anything with the bling factor sold like hot cakes.

There were two distinct groups of visitors to the fair. Romany Gypsy and Irish Travellers. They were like chalk and cheese. The Romany families were immaculate, dressed in tweed suits and handmade leather boots, and their children all wore matching outfits. Serious money had been spent and it showed. They looked happy. The children were smiling, glad to be out with their parents. The family would approach the stall and make polite conversation, asking to which family I was connected, then warmly wishing us luck for the day ahead.

Then came the Irish Travellers. Generalizations are always unfair, but it was hard to change my attitude about these folk from my direct experience. Men in tracksuit bottoms and V-neck sweaters. Girls in Day-glo bikini tops with bare bellies overhanging short shorts. What a spectacle. Rude, brash, their grabbing hands trying to confuse and distract you while others tried to pinch something. Luckily we'd tied the bags on the rails and not just hung them, which made it impossible just to snatch one and disappear, yet Andy and I needed eyes in the back of our heads. They quickly identified us as gorgias and tried every trick in the book to fiddle us out of goods or money. The two groups really were like oil and water.

As the day went on I'm sorry to say I felt a growing dislike for the Travellers, but my attitude towards the genuine Gypsy folk was changing. I shared their anger at the surveillance helicopter and the heavy-handed way the event had been policed. This was an important part of their culture, and the authorities were trying to crush it. The weary look of defeat on their faces as they watched the hovering helicopter, and the confusion' on the children's faces as their parents tried to explain, was sad to see. Why not just leave them alone and let them enjoy their day? If they had a fight, it would be among themselves, and if they wanted to sell hooky goods, it was to each other. The police crackdown, from what I could tell, was the deliberate oppression of a culture, of a tradition that had taken place here for hundreds of years.

The political elite would never tolerate such bias against a Gay Pride march or one of the many religious groups enjoying public festivals, yet for them bullying Gypsies seemed fair game.

Later on, the younger lads started driving the luxury cars round and round the fair, churning up the mud. Music pumping, they crawled and slid between the stalls, their hard stares replaced with big grins if you gave them the thumbs-up to acknowledge their car.

The owner of the land, and the organizer of the horse fair, came up and stood beside me. He was always followed by an entourage of younger lads, and whether they were there to do his bidding if he saw a job that needed doing, or were simply watching over the head of their family, it wasn't clear. One thing was for sure: he was a respected Gypsy elder, and I felt pleased that he was prepared to share idle chat with me.

'Things are very different now,' he said. 'Years ago these young fellas would be riding the ponies and the horses through here.' He raised a hand towards one of the Mercedes churning up the paddock. 'They'd be showing folk what horses they'd bred or traded, and getting ready for races to the village pub and back.'

Harness racing, better known in Gypsy circles as

trotting, is a centuries-old tradition of racing horses attached to a two-wheel cart. Thousands of pounds can be wagered on these illegal street races, often taking place on the public highway with hundreds of Travellers watching. Police had cracked down on those events, citing the danger to other road-users, and the animals themselves – the RSPCA had also campaigned against it. Anyway, there was none of that today, not at this modern horse fair.

'Now it's fancy cars with music blasting out.' The Gypsy elder shook his head as another sports car came wheel-spinning by.

'You've seen some changes, then?'

'More than you'd guess, young fella, more than you'd guess.' He turned and looked me in the eye. 'This fair will die with me. Everything has its time.' He reached out and shook my hand. 'Luck be with you.'

I watched him wander over to the next stall, checking in on the traders to ask how they'd fared. As I watched him chatting and shaking hands, wishing folk luck, I realized that this was better treatment than I'd received at any of the professionally run county fairs. He was a gentleman, and I'd gained an instant respect and liking for him.

The fair was drawing to a close. The whine of sports cars turning slow doughnuts in the mud was quietening, and we hadn't sold anything for an hour. It was time to head home. We broke the stall down and loaded up. It was touch and go getting out of the boggy field, and it was almost three in the morning when we drove back into Hope Valley. We hadn't stopped talking all the way there. For both of us it had been a real eye-opener. An insight into Gypsy life. An experience I'd enjoyed immensely.

25

It was a sad day. The fateful departure from the valley that I loved so much had finally arrived. I held things together pretty well until I popped round to say goodbye to my elderly neighbour, Josie. She was a wonderful lady, and had been a teacher and a magistrate in the course of her long career, and much loved by all. Saying goodbye on her doorstep was hard. In my mind she'd become a surrogate grandparent, and I knew I'd miss her. I remembered the first time we'd met as I was cleaning the house. She'd simply popped her white-crowned head through the window with a cheery hello and the offer of a cuppa. Over the length of my time there we'd spent hours chatting about her memories and the rich life she'd enjoyed. She reminded me so much of my own departed grandparents. I'd tried my best to be a good neighbour, clearing the snow off her path in winter, and fetching in coal or firewood. We'd become friends and it hurt to say goodbye. I gave her a hug and couldn't speak. She knew I was sad, and that upset her in turn. As I pulled away with my trailer hitched behind, she raised a hand in farewell. It was the last time I saw her.

Since my early childhood trips to Derbyshire the Peak District had earned itself a special place in my heart. As I drove away, remembering the happy times, every landmark seemed to cause physical pain. One of the main features in Hope Valley is the massive cement works. A gargantuan concrete building towering out of the meadows surrounding Hope village. It may be just a chimney poking up into the clouds, some would even say an eyesore, and visible for miles in every direction, but to me it was beautiful. Coming through Hathersage on our way into the valley, we'd crane our necks to get the first view of the chimney stack. Our parents had told me and my brother it was the weather factory, and that the sunshine on our holiday depended on it pumping out clouds or not. And we'd believed them. It was a happy coincidence that the ever-present vapour billowing out of the top was only visible on cloudy days.

Next I passed the ruins of the public swimming pool by the Rising Sun Hotel. As children we'd go for a dip, have a packet of Snaps for fourpence, get dressed in our Paisley pyjamas, and leap straight into our sleeping bags on returning to the campsite.

The open-air pool at Hathersage, the signs for the café at Grindleford Station, Chatsworth House: every landmark was a painful reminder of happier times. I felt sick, and the four-hour journey to Elmstead Market was torture.

Over the previous weeks I'd been staying at Eddie's house, working on the plot with him and enjoying a beer after a day's hard grafting. He certainly liked a tinny or two in the evenings, and I struggled to keep up with him sometimes.

As we cleared the space I left a row of scrub and bushes along the front to offer some privacy. Near these was an old ditch that had mostly collapsed in on itself so I used the digger to clear it out. As soon as we started digging we found red warning signs, 'Caution, live electricity', buried underground. 'Whoa, stop!' I shouted, well aware of the dangers of hitting underground services. Carefully, with a spade, I investigated what was buried there. A black cable as thick as my thumb ran twenty feet into the plot and just ended. I ran and got a tester. It was live. It had been a close shave with the digger, but raised the question as to why there was a random live cable on the land.

It turned out to be an old supply for an illuminated sign on the edge of the village. They had simply buried the cable rather than climb the pole and disconnect it properly. After I'd made a couple of calls, engineers rocked up and the live cable was no more. Then I realized what I'd done. I had just surrendered a free supply of electricity that would never have been traced. As various members of Rhoda's family heard the story, their laughter gave little comfort. We were stuck with the generator. I was crushed. I never lost the tag of the Gorgia Who Lost Free Electric for his Home.

Joe had dragged all the bushes and trees into a huge pile, at least a hundred foot long by thirty across. The plan was to douse it in petrol and set light to it all. That seemed easy enough in principle, but I hadn't really thought through how big this blaze would get. I made use of a gentle morning breeze to encourage the flames down the length of the pile, and within the hour a sudden gale had turned a controlled burn into a furnace. The flames were leaping twenty feet into the air, and the heat was so intense that I couldn't get anywhere near it to drag bits out or keep it under control. Fortunately the size of the plot had allowed me to build the fire far enough from the trailer for it to be safe. A plume of smoke was extending ever upwards, clearly marking the source of the burning. For thirty hours I watched over that fire, buckets of water spread around the plot, ready to dampen any flying embers or sparks. I should have split the fuel into at least four separate stacks, but lack of energy and common sense had prevailed.

I suppose it was another blaze I was lucky not to have been reported for. I was expecting the fire brigade or the police at any moment, and after a very nervous day and a half I was able to fold the fire in on itself and let the last bits burn out.

Another thing I had to do was build a fence across the bottom of the plot where our land ended and a neighbour's lawn began. I'm not one for doing things by halves, and as this was going to be our home for years I invested in concrete posts, upped the dimensions of the wood in every respect, and hand nailed on the individual boards. Four days' hard work but I was pleased with the end result. It looked strong and well made, like the fort it would ultimately become.

I'd laid in some ground pipes from the caravan to a septic tank further down the plot. I'd never done that before so relied on advice from Eddie and a few others. With sewage pipes you need to be within a certain angle. Too level and the solids just sit there, too steep and the liquids race away leaving the solids behind. The waste has to float down on its merry way. Testing I'd got my maths correct is not something I'd ever want to do again, and certainly not in daylight.

On my first attempt at burying the septic tank it had simply popped back up as I hadn't put any water in the tank to hold it in the ground. I also drove up to North Lincolnshire and bought an old water bowser, which held a thousand litres. It was no good for drinking from, but okay to use for building work. When I next put the septic tank in the ground I filled it with water as I bedded it in, then laid a concrete collar around the top. It stayed underground, much to my relief. I now realized that not having access to water on the plot was going to be an ongoing problem.

I was introduced to my other neighbours. Next door was a care home with about a dozen patients as residents, who needed constant care. After chatting with staff I was told they sedated the patients except for about an hour a day. It didn't seem right to me, but I guess it conformed to regulations. Until I'd arrived on the adjacent plot there'd been no boundary fence between their gardens and the wasteland that had become Rhoda's and my plot. But now a fence was needed down the long side of the plot to match the one I had built at the bottom, and I couldn't see why I should pay for it. I asked the owner a few times but he was famous for being tight with money, so I called the authority responsible for monitoring the care home. I pretended to be a concerned parent of one of the patients. I voiced my fears that now the adjoining plot had been cleared my child, among the other patients, could just wander into next door's property. I added my concerns about privacy and dignity for the patients. Within two weeks a contractor was installing a boundary fence. Result.

Obviously we needed services connecting to the trailer – water and electricity. But neither company would supply them without us having a postal address. And I couldn't get a postal address without permission from the council for a change of use to residential. And that was where my latest troubles began.

It soon became apparent that there was no way the council would give us a change of use on the site. They knew it was Gypsy land. Every time I went there I was given new reasons why we couldn't have a postal address. It was beyond frustrating. We had to manage without water or electricity in the short term until I had exhausted every option to get them connected.

The generator I'd rigged up gave us lights and television for a few hours in the evenings. It also ran a fridge so we could chill milk, cheese and other perishables. But only while it was running. The constant noise was maddening, and only by turning up the telly was it possible to ignore the thudding engine.

The wood-burner I fitted was a saviour in the cold

months. It pumped out eight kilowatts of heat, at least double what was needed in the trailer, and it kept us as warm as toast. One of Rhoda's great-uncles had a deal going with a company near Clacton that made roof joists. He collected all the offcuts and saved them having to dispose of the waste. I suppose he was paid a small fee for taking it all away, and a bigger fee for delivering it as firewood. A true Romany entrepreneur. And it was perfect for us. I'd built a lean-to beside the container to house the generator and it was stacked with firewood ready for the winter ahead. Nothing beats a real fire for lifting your spirits. So the trailer was liveable, but not ideal by any standards. It was such a drastic change from the house, and I was trying to stay positive, but it was an ongoing effort to be optimistic about our situation.

Our main problem was water or, rather, the lack of it. Since the installation of water meters few folk let you fill a container for free. My neighbours had called the owner of the care home when I'd asked about filling a jerry can so we could have a cup of tea, and he'd said no. Years ago the painted Gypsy wagons set stainless-steel dairy churns on the back to carry their water. That's another reason life on the road is so hard in modern times. Where do you go for clean water?

My main source was from a standpipe intended for dog-walkers in Brightlingsea. I'd go there three times a week and fill camping water containers, which I would then use for washing and cooking. Once I had the toilet waste piped up, I started collecting rain water, which I used to flush the toilet. Life was hard, and I realized how much I'd taken for granted before this latest move, like turning on a light switch or a tap.

I could see Rhoda was struggling as well. The irony of my predicament had not escaped me. I was living in a caravan in the most basic of circumstances. When I'd lived in a comfortable house and had a comfortable job, I'd moved Travellers on by setting fire to their caravans. It was as if Fate was teaching me the error of my earlier years. My prejudiced opinion, my summary judgement of a group of people had been wrong. I knew that now. The only real difference was that the landowner was happy for us to be there.

26

Since our arrival on the plot we'd been visited by most of Rhoda's extended family. I hadn't known just how large the numbers were on her mother's side. Romany religious leanings are towards the Catholic Church, and birth control is frowned upon. There's great pride in having a large family, along with the care and comfort expected in later life from the support of so many children.

Rhoda's mother was one of six daughters Riley and Tillie had raised on the road in the traditional Gypsy way. All the girls had grown up with a love of over-the-top style in wardrobe and décor. I could see it in Rhoda's genes: she was clad from head to toe in leopard-print clothes, with jewel-encrusted hands and an obsession with anything Disney. Although none of her mother's generation now lived in caravans, they still enjoyed the traditional Italian furniture, and the ever-present Crown Derby china. Her family had homes spread from near Ipswich down to the south of Colchester, and the only remaining family member preferring to live in a caravan was her grandfather, Riley. And, of course, us.

Meeting Rhoda's aunts was like a looking glass into the future. As I was introduced to them one by one it was clear they were sisters, hair freshly done, brightly manicured nails, and dressed up to the nines just for popping to the supermarket, or visiting the plot. They all offered help and advice on how to get by on the site, along with some ribbing for passing up on the free electric. But mostly it was much appreciated help and encouragement.

In our first weeks on the site we went over to Ardleigh car-boot sale on a Sunday morning. It's one of the biggest in Essex, with hundreds of stalls selling a plethora of things, from fresh food to vehicles. A few of Rhoda's aunts had stalls there, and her grandparents were regular fixtures. One of her aunts specialized in kids' stuff – prams, car seats, garden toys and other child-related bits and pieces. She'd buy them early, off less-experienced stallholders, then mark up a hefty profit upon resale. It had become an obsession with her, and I'd seen the storage sheds back at her home stacked with thousands of items. I tried to sell our handbags there one week, but with it being a car boot rather than a proper market everybody wanted them for fifty pence, and after Rhoda had bought a few bits and pieces for herself, we went home with more stuff than we'd taken there.

Wandering round Ardleigh I was able to see which stalls were run by Travellers and which by regular folk just doing a one-off sale to shift unwanted stuff. The Travellers had their regular spots, turning up before dawn to get first access and set up early. They'd have a regular line of one product, anything from light-bulbs to printer paper. The other half of their stall might be house-clearance items, although whether the previous owners had consented to their removal tended to be unclear. I'd heard that members of extended families from other ends of the country would meet up to exchange stolen goods to avoid local victims tracking down their possessions. And there were always some bits and pieces of absolute rubbish, items that other car-booters had dumped rather than reload and drive away. The Traveller thinking was that somebody, some day, would eventually part with a few pennies or pounds for what was essentially a piece of junk. In a way, it was re-cycling at its best.

Still, the easiest way to spot a Traveller was from how they worked the punters. They grafted at selling, and there was no hesitancy or humility in engaging browsers and trying to secure a sale. Regular folk are quite shy about trying to sell something they no longer want, and almost embarrassed about asking for money for something they've labelled rubbish. Travellers have no qualms, and quickly launch into a confident haggle.

Rhoda loved it, chatting with fellow Gypsies and catching up on news. We always came home with some bargain or other, or a bit of tat we could hardly afford, no matter what price she'd haggled.

I desperately needed an income. The work I'd done on the plot, then the purchase of the caravan and the con-tainer had pretty much wiped out any funds I'd salvaged from Derbyshire. A common topic of conversation was breeding dogs. Nearly all of Rhoda's relatives kept dif-ferent breeds and it seemed like easy money. I had my

Alfie and he was like family to me, but it soon became apparent that my attitude to dogs was a complete contrast to that of the wider Travelling community. The worst type of breeders regarded the dogs simply as a source of income, and there was no affection for the animal as a family pet.

One of Rhoda's many cousins had explained how some dogs were treated. The breeding bitches were bred to near death, exhausted by litter after litter after litter. Regular folk would respond to adverts on Gumtree or pet-listing sites on social media, and if they agreed a viewing the bitch and her puppies would be delivered to a house half an hour before the customer's arrival. The living room would be dressed like a film set. Framed photos of the breed being sold would go up on the walls, and the patter would begin: 'This is our family pet. These are her first pups. We were advised to let her have just one litter.'

The punter would part with anything from one to two thousand pounds, and leave with a puppy. Kennel Club papers were forged and issued, and as soon as the new owners had gone, the next bitch and her litter would be collected. It was like a conveyor belt. New photos on the wall, and rehearsed sales patter about how the dog was their beloved family pet.

English bulldogs, Italian greyhounds, pugs and Chihuahuas. Thousands and thousands of pounds were changing hands, all tax free. If the puppies got too old to sell and they weren't required for breeding, they were destroyed, drowned, their small carcasses thrown on a fire. Why keep them if they weren't selling? They'd cost money to feed.

I wanted no part of that barbaric breeding factory, and the dog business was a source of arguments between Rhoda and me.

Riley and Tillie, Rhoda's grandparents, were regular visitors to our trailer. There was an obvious bond between Rhoda and her grandfather, and it was lovely to see them laughing together. I took an instant liking to Riley. He was a big man even then in his later years, broad shoulders and large hands, hardened after a lifetime of graft. I always felt Riley liked visiting the trailer because he felt comfortable there. He'd just started staying in a house recently due to ill health, but before that he'd been in his caravan on his plot near Needham Market, thirty-odd acres of land given over to growing Christmas trees and firewood. Riley's caravan was a simple tourer that he'd pulled deep into the woods, well away from prying eyes. It was a basic existence, but he'd been happy there.

Riley loved telling stories of times gone by. Life had changed dramatically for him over the years but he still had a ready smile and had kept his sense of humour. I always enjoyed his visits because seeing him would lift Rhoda's spirits. We were struggling since the move down, not just financially, but living in those conditions was harder than we'd expected.

I was talking to Riley one day about the council and their efforts to move us on.

'They won't do anything,' he reassured us. 'Not enough people or time. They'll just keep sending you letters, which you must ignore. Don't join in the conversation. Once you answer they can say you said this or you said that. Best to ignore them. They don't know how to handle silence, and you end up being left alone. They've been trying to stop me living in the woods for years. No chance.'

He was a veteran of many similar disputes, and had learnt over the years that the best way forward was to smile and say as little as possible. Time would prove him correct. I found myself liking Riley more and more. He seemed to be an island of calm in a sea of madness.

I sold the van I'd kept from Saracen and bought an old Land Rover. Making use of the time I had, I restored it, spraying it matt black with a bright orange bonnet and grille. The finishing touch was the word 'Norfolk' across the front where it normally said 'Land Rover'. A remarkable number of people asked me about this Norfolk model and, depending on my mood, I'd tell them a variety of tall stories. But it did look good. And I loved it. The problem was keeping it running when I had no money. Things like tax and insurance, the MOT, were just put on hold.

'I'll get them next week,' I found myself saying. Week after week. No cash usually meant no car. Legally, anyway.

But my approach to the law had evolved, and desperate

times called for desperate measures. Prohibited things I'd never considered doing I now readily accepted. Driving illegally was just one of my daily transgressions. I knew police cars had cameras fitted with number-plate recognition to check things like insurance or MOT, so if a patrol car joined the traffic behind me I simply pulled over to let them by. To start with I felt nervous every time I put the key into the ignition, but it soon became an automatic habit, forced on me by a financial burden: I was skint.

Eddie, whom I'd stayed with in those early weeks when I first arrived in Essex, came to the rescue with a job for me. He had a contract with Felixstowe docks doing groundworks and block paving, and as he could use a willing pair of hands he offered me a few days' labour. Now I was driving in and out of one of the most secure locations in the country in an illegal vehicle. Despite my increasing nonchalance at breaking the law I always felt tense passing the constant police presence at the gates.

Felixstowe docks fascinated me. Once I'd sat through the most basic of safety videos I was given a photo identity card and could roam the site with a fair degree of freedom. We were told to drive on the frontage area only when we really had to, but I often found myself enjoying a run under the huge gantry cranes. With my engineering background I was drawn to the cranes, their sheer scale, towering up into the sky, unloading containers as if they were cigarette packets. The crane drivers could work only limited shifts because they had to lie face down to manoeuvre the containers, with the ships and lorries far below. If a fire broke out there was a cable they could clip to and just jump. Their body weight and speed of fall operated the drum brakes to slow their descent safely. All the drivers performed a practice jump as part of their training, and I fancied a go but doubted I'd ever get permission.

Driving on the wharf I got a sense of the mammoth scale of the ships and their cargo. The docks were successful because they could process some of the biggest vessels in the world, coming in from China, India, everywhere. There was a constant queue of lorries waiting below to take each container away to its final destination. A few of the cranes sat over a rail siding and the containers would leave in a long line pulled by a huge diesel locomotive. I loved every part of it, and as well as earning some precious cash, it gave me time away from day to day life in the trailer, and a little space to daydream.

Still, we were there to replace sections of block paving. Proper graft. Because the whole dock area was on reclaimed land it would sink in certain areas, and we were there to replace it as new. Christ alone knew how many blocks made up the whole dock area – it seemed like millions.

I enjoyed the work, and most lunchtimes we'd go to a local pub for a quick pint or three, and on a hot day we'd drive to Felixstowe beach for a swim. Walking out on the sand, pulling off our hi-vis vests and steel toe-capped boots to dive into the sea in our boxers, was a real treat in the summer.

It felt like things were starting to level out. Life was looking up again, just. I was earning money, not a lot but enough to pay for food and to get by. The depressing thing was that it didn't seem to matter what I earned, we were always broke and living a hand-to-mouth existence. I'd mostly got used to driving around illegally, and it was amazing how after a few weeks of anxiety it became so easy to break the law.

It was a state of mind that financial necessity created. And I was comfortable with it, knowing that more folk than I'd ever imagined bent the rules. How else was I supposed to get by?

I was spending more and more time with different members of Rhoda's family. They always had some advice or an offer of help to improve our situation. Gypsies lived in the system but on their own terms. Bending the rules was encouraged, not judged or frowned upon. In the past I'd always tried to be an upstanding member of society, a contributor to the system I believed in. I paid my taxes, abided by the law, and only broke it when the legal system failed to protect the community.

That approach was changing now I'd been left high and dry. There was no safety net for me. I'd been into the benefits office, which had hurt my pride: Jobseekers' Allowance for four weeks, then take a job at McDonald's or get lost. Hardly a return for twenty-five years of tax and National Insurance payments. I could earn more cash in a day on a building site or a private fencing job than a month's Jobseekers' Allowance was worth so it was a no-brainer. It was the black economy for me now. I had to adapt and get by as best I could. So there I was, happily living outside the law. Driving with no insurance, a dodgy MOT, using red diesel. Earning cash whenever possible. I gradually adopted the attitude that I was outside accepted society, so why should I pay towards it?

A regular sounding post for my frustrations was Riley. 'All I wanted was to be left alone in peace,' he was telling me, of his recent years living in his woodland near Needham Market. 'But the council just kept on and on.'

Despite Tillie having a house in Ipswich Riley had preferred the traditional lifestyle, staying in his trailer. After ill-health had finally forced him to join his wife in the house, he still spent as much time as he could visiting the site. Throughout his time in the woods he'd suffered years of petty harassment aimed at stopping him living there.

'Why wouldn't they just let you be?' I asked. 'You owned the land. What business was it of anyone's what you did up there?'

'It's about control,' Riley explained. 'Councils and authorities need to feel like they control you and your life. They don't like Gypsy folk because they can't control us.'

Riley had told me how he'd wander round the woodland trails, shooting a pheasant or some rabbits to eat. But the police had eventually taken his shotgun, as it had been impossible for him to comply with gun-storage regulations, such as fixed steel cabinets, when he lived in a caravan.

As the weeks rolled by and I listened to Riley talking about his life, I could see the appeal more and more. That feeling of freedom from the state, nobody looking over your shoulder, telling you what to do and how to live. Freedom from the rules. A way of life that was becoming evermore enticing.

27

As life was improving for me, Rhoda seemed to be struggling more. My love for outdoor pursuits, like camping and backpacking, had helped me cope with realities in the trailer. But for her it was a different matter. The lack of a shower, not being able to wash easily or dry her hair, keep her clothes nice, weighed her down as time went by.

'I'm not feeling right,' Rhoda said one morning. Her tone made me sit up and take her seriously. She didn't look well. Her skin was patchy, and she looked swollen around her neck and wrists.

'We need to get you to the doctor,' I said. 'You don't look too sharp.'

As luck would have it I had a few days off, so I took her up to the local surgery. By now Rhoda was also complaining about stiffness in her joints. Walking was uncomfortable, and her skin was getting worse. Maybe it was because she normally looked so perfect that I feared the worst.

After we'd spent an hour at the local surgery, the doctor called the hospital in Colchester. We were to head up there for some blood tests. I held Rhoda's hand as we walked into the hospital. She normally had the warmest, softest hands, but not today. They were cold and clammy, and she was shuffling rather than walking.

'You'll be fine,' I reassured her. 'They'll figure this out in no time.'

She raised a small smile, and despite looking grey around the gills, she was still beautiful.

They sat her in a wheelchair and off she went for tests. After a couple of hours she was admitted to stay overnight.

'What things do you want me to bring back?' I asked, trying to sound full of confidence that everything was going to be fine. Rhoda reeled off a list, phone charger, toothbrush, underwear, and a few other things. I went home promising to be back later.

The first person I called was Tony, as I knew how much he loved his daughter and would want to know she was in hospital. We had a chat and he said to keep him updated. We said goodbye and I got into the Land Rover to head back across Colchester. The emotions racing through my mind were overwhelming. I felt as though I'd already lost so much. Surely I wasn't going to lose Rhoda as well. This couldn't be happening. Life just kept kicking me in the nuts. The journey back to the locked gates of the plot was at least twenty minutes, yet I couldn't remember twenty seconds of actually driving. I felt sick, empty and beaten. Thoroughly beaten. I'd been crying without knowing it. This was proving more than my fragile mind could deal with.

I opened the door to the trailer and there was Alfie, just standing there. Normally he'd have bowled past me without a second glance, off to piss and chase the pigeons that had been taunting him through the windows. But that day he simply stood and stared at me. I dropped to my knees and he curled his head around my neck and wagged his body steadily back and forth. He knew. He sensed the raw emotion in my face. I'd drawn comfort many times before from his huge, warm frame, and his love lifted me once again. I took him for a walk across the fields, and instead of bounding away as usual he stayed close to me. I've no idea how to explain the link between a dog and its owner, but it's a real thing.

An hour with Alfie got me back into gear and I headed to the trailer in a better state of mind.

Later that evening I was back up at the hospital with Rhoda's bag packed with all the things she'd requested. 'Any news?' I asked nervously.

'It's to do with my white blood cells,' she explained. 'My count is too low.'

After some small-talk about the news, who I'd called and told about her being admitted to hospital, I searched out a doctor to see if I could get more detail on her condition. I found the consultant directly involved with Rhoda's treatment.

'The symptoms are related to leukaemia,' he stated flatly, as if he were commenting on the weather.

And my world slipped sideways. I could feel the blood pulsing through my chest. I felt dizzy. 'Leukaemia?' I whispered.

'Yes, but until we do more tests we won't know the full diagnosis.'

Of course medical professionals are taught to deliver news in a straight and honest manner, but this was hard to take. I walked back to Rhoda and could see she'd been crying. Her legs were wrapped in those elastic stockings, and her skin had angry red blotches all over it. I sat and held her hand.

Within minutes Tony had arrived. 'All right, my girl?' he asked, voice thick with emotion. No parent likes to see their child in distress, and Tony was no different. I knew he hated hospitals, most Travellers do, with a natural mistrust for anything that was part of the system. I left them to talk and went to get some coffee.

This was to be our routine for at least a week. I would be there and Tony would arrive, making the journey down every day to see his daughter. After a few days the staff at the hospital gave us some good news. It wasn't full-blown leukaemia, but a related condition: familial Mediterranean fever, an illness peculiar to Romany Gypsies. I'd wondered why the doctors had asked such detailed questions about Rhoda's heritage, her family history and origins. It had allowed them to track down her diagnosis correctly. Well, at least we now knew what was wrong, and that it could be controlled with medication. She'd never beat it, there's no cure, but she could manage it and live with it.

I was there for my usual visit when my phone rang. An unknown number. I answered, sitting beside Rhoda's bed.

'Hello, Mike here,' I said, into the handset.

A clearly upset female voice replied. 'Mike, it's Annie.' Annie was one of Rhoda's aunts. 'He's died. Can you tell Rhoda her granddad has died?'

Modern phones have loudspeakers, and my impaired hearing – a legacy, I imagine, of my years as a DJ – meant mine was set on full. Rhoda heard every word.

'You mean Riley?' I asked.

'Yes. They found him at home after the car boot at Ardleigh. He was sat in his chair when Mum got back.'

I thanked her for letting us know and ended the call. I turned to look at Rhoda. Just how she felt at that moment was impossible for anyone to grasp. After weeks of ill health, tests, and dealing with the possibility of leukaemia, she'd now lost someone she loved dearly.

Tears rolled down her face. 'No, no, no, no,' she cried, as if refusing to accept what had happened. I held her hands as she cried, a low moaning split by racking sobs that shook her whole body. I'd never witnessed grief like that, and it had a profound effect on me. Tony arrived in the midst of this scene and I quickly explained what had happened. He comforted his daughter and I went for help. Within minutes Rhoda was sedated and went to sleep. My heart was broken for her. I'd only known Riley a matter of months but had grown to like and respect him. He was leaving a massive gap in his family's life.

28

The day of the funeral quickly arrived. Determined to attend the service, Rhoda had discharged herself from hospital only the day before. Her symptoms were debilitating fatigue, painful joints and skin reacting in angry red patches. And now her eyes were dark and puffy from crying over the death of her beloved grandfather, and lack of sleep. Being confined to a hospital bed while the rest of the family comforted each other and made funeral plans had taken its toll.

After I'd woken up and brewed us a cup of tea, I went out to the container, gathered a dozen items for Rhoda, a shirt and a suit for myself, and headed back to the caravan.

Rhoda hadn't moved, and I could see fresh tears on her face.

'Come on, it'll be okay.' I tried to soothe her. 'Be strong. How are your legs?'

I knew how she felt about people seeing her not at her best. Especially the people who'd be there today. Any Gypsy gathering is a chance to display your wealth and look your best, funerals included.

'I'll be okay,' she whispered.

'It's a beautiful day,' I said, wiping the condensation

off the huge windows so she could see the sunshine spread across the fields. 'Fancy a bacon sandwich?'

She nodded, so I relit the gas hob, got some bacon from the fridge, and replaced the kettle for a second cup of tea. The thick sandwich eased the empty nervousness from my stomach, and I hoped it would make Rhoda feel better as well.

I had to fire up the generator so I could iron a shirt and press my suit. The generator had been stolen from a hire company somewhere in Kent. Probably from a yard just like the one I used to own. A flash of pink paint denoted the company branding beside a registration number that had been ground away. It was a Honda, the only brand worth having, a reliable workhorse. I'd tried to muffle the noise it made but the steady thrumming of the engine permeated every fibre of me and I hated it. Most Gypsies bury them underground in a pit if they're staying somewhere for a long time. I guess it was my reluctance to admit I was stuck there for a while that had stopped me doing that.

Coughing from the cloud of fumes, I emerged from the wood store that housed the generator to see Alfie sitting waiting for his breakfast. His food was in a plastic bin with a lid clamped firmly in place. Rats were everywhere in the Essex countryside. After feeding and making a fuss of him, I headed back in to get my clothes ready. Rhoda had some music on to drown out the generator. It helped, but I could still hear it. I'd brought the iron in from the container and spread a towel on the table, my makeshift ironing board. I poured some bottled water into the iron and flicked the switch.

The generator promptly died, juddering to a halt in the abrupt silence as the music stopped and the lights went out.

In that moment of darkness I thought back to the first attack on the caravans, crawling through the hedge, bottles of petrol in hand, ready to throw fire at a trailer just like this one. We'd crawled into a pitch-black field next to the caravans. No lights. The silence was total. Not even a dog. Where were the dogs? Gypsies always kept dogs on site.

It had been cold enough to see our breath, hanging like shrouds over our helmeted faces. Our disguises.

'Fuck,' I muttered, bringing myself back to the here and now, the day of a Gypsy funeral.

I went outside to restart the generator. The trip had gone, caused by the surge required to power the iron. More noise, more fumes, and then it was running again. On the way back in I saw Alfie patrolling the perimeter of the plot, standing on his hind legs against a tree, chasing squirrels he'd disturbed from gathering supplies for the winter. I smiled, a moment of relief from the tension of the day.

As soon as I switched on the iron the generator died. Again.

'You'll have to wear them as they are,' snapped Rhoda.

'It'll work. We just have to switch everything else off for a minute.'

I went round switching off the lights, the radio, the fridge. I unplugged my battery drills that I always had on charge while it was running. Even the mobile-phone chargers came out of their sockets. This time it worked, and ten minutes later my shirt and suit hung ready to go.

'If there's nothing else you need I'm going to take Alfie for a run.'

Rhoda was focused on the mirror, starting her make-up process. 'I'm fine,' she replied, her voice thick with emotion. I gave her a quick hug and a kiss, and headed outside.

As soon as Alfie saw the lead he went crazy, barking and jumping up on all fours. Walking him cleared my mind and helped me relax. The sun was fully up, and I could feel the heat through my rugby shirt. In the distance I could hear a siren droning towards the coast.

I walked along the road before I turned up the regular farm track with Alfie. As I closed the gates a car drove past, faces at the window full of judgement at the trailer on the plot. Me. I'd never been on the receiving end of bigoted intolerance before, yet here in this village it was a daily event. I'd been tagged as a Traveller, a Gypsy, living in a trailer on the edge of the village. Did it upset me more because it was a new experience or because they were wrong? Or were they right? Fuck them. I was half-way down the lane now, Alfie enjoying himself bounding through the long grass and running up and down the ditch. The farmer was driving towards me, but Alfie had always been very aware of cars so I let him be.

The farmer pulled up beside me in his Land Rover Discovery. 'Your dog should be on a lead,' he bellowed.

'He's fine,' I replied. 'There's no livestock, and if there was he wouldn't go near it.'

'You should have him under control,' he snapped, starting to open his door. 'I know who you are,' he added, his tone full of contempt.

'He's under more control than your mouth,' I countered. 'And I'd stay in your car if I were you.' This wasn't a good day to pick a fight. 'Get back in and fuck off.'

He paused. His face was red with temper but he'd heard the edge in my voice and decided against further provocation. He slammed the door and accelerated away, stones pattering against my legs. My fists had been clenched, and I slowly unwound the white knuckles.

Once upon a time I'd stood beside a farmer who had threatened Travellers with a shotgun. Now I was threatening to fight a farmer because I was a Traveller. My life had gone full circle.

After I got back from walking Alfie, and I'd calmed down from my altercation with the farmer, I opened the trailer door. Rhoda was ready, and the results were incredible. Her transformation from first thing that morning was total. She looked stunning.

'You look lovely,' I told her. 'Beautiful. What time do you want to make a move?'

I had to have a strip wash and get dressed – thirty minutes would cover it easily. I put a large pan of water on the gas hob and started undressing, ready for a scrub down. As I washed I couldn't get the thought out of my head. Would anybody recognize me? Maybe someone would overhear a snippet of conversation and guess who I was. Stop worrying, I told myself. It was time to get dressed and get on with the day.

I'd already cleaned the car, and despite its age it looked smart enough. Rhoda had made it clear that we'd be judged on our appearances, so it had to be her Mercedes rather than my battered Land Rover. Rhoda was resplendent in jet black Karen Millen from head to toe. I had on a dark navy suit with a black tie. Not that I'd get home with it in such good condition.

As we drove into the cemetery all I could see were rows of Range Rovers, Rolls-Royces, a few Bentleys and other top-of-the-range motors. It looked like a luxury car forecourt. Groups of people stood around the entrance – easily two hundred were gathered already. The men's outfits varied from expensive suits to plain jumpers with a tie, and most of the women seemed to be adorned in some sort of animal print. It was Gypsy bling. Gold, jewels and diamanté everywhere I looked. I knew that the history of the men's gold earring was to show they carried at least that value on their person, and apparently it's the same with sailors. Hands were shaken and quiet conversations took place. Rhoda was moving from group to group, hugs and commiserations from everyone she spoke with. I hung back, not wanting to intrude. A few family members wandered over and said brief greetings, and I expressed my sadness over their loss.

Winding its way towards us, the hearse was followed by a black car carrying Riley's widow and favoured daughters. We were guided into position and gently talked through carrying the coffin into the chapel. Riley had been a big man during his living years and the weight came as a surprise. After placing the coffin on the trestles I walked towards the back. Rhoda had taken a seat near the front but I didn't feel it was my place to sit there. I was fielding lots of curious looks, and responded with a tight smile and a curt nod. I felt strangely isolated and vulnerable. If any of those Travellers knew my history there would be hell to pay, and that knowledge sank in my gut like a stone.

The service was story after story about the big man: how he used to import horses by loading every deck of a ferry from Ireland, then drive the herd across England. He'd been in a dozen different prisons, and I was surprised to hear the chaplain regale the mourners with tales of theft and fighting. Then I realized that he was conversant with Gypsy funerals, and that this was a popular cemetery among the community. Again, I felt out of place, an imposter. A letter from Riley's grandson was read out – he'd not been allowed out of jail to attend as he was considered a flight risk. His letter spoke of his grief, and the promises to be a better person out of respect to his grandfather.

Sombre-faced and in immaculate suits, the pall bearers carried Riley back to the waiting hearse. It was a two-hundred-yard walk to the graveside and I joined the crowd, more people freely saying hello, commenting on the service or making small-talk about Riley and their part in his life.

Then, as the coffin was lowered by ropes into the grave, a strange thing happened. All the men, and some of the boys, started taking off their ties and waistcoats and throwing them into the hole on top of the coffin. I looked at Rhoda, uncertain of the etiquette. She nodded. So I threw a perfectly good tie into the grave – nothing compared to the expensive waistcoats reducing the smart three-piece suits to two. I later found out it's considered bad luck to wear these items again after attending a Gypsy funeral.

Next a dumper approached, the bucket full of top soil. I was handed a shovel. There were at least a dozen being given out and I was near the front, looking confused. I watched as other men started to fill the grave, hollow thuds softened by the layer of ties and waistcoats on the coffin. I handed my jacket to Rhoda and joined in. I felt honoured to be one of the first group, and I was gripped by an urge to be accepted, to be safe among the very community I'd battled with.

It was the custom to fill the grave straight away so that nobody could rob the coffin. I smiled to myself thinking about the claims of wealth to be made about the contents of Riley's coffin. Knowing his wife, I doubted there was anything of any value in the ground. But the legend would grow of gold watches and coins she'd claim to have placed inside.

Finally the grave was topped off, the mound covered with a piece of artificial grass. I was pleased to be asked to help lift the flowers on to the top. There were spectacular wreaths made to represent his Gypsy life, everything from horseshoes and a large Gypsy wagon drawn by a pony, to pheasants and guns.

The wake was to take place at the Leather Bottle, a pub owned by a Gypsy and good friend of Riley's. The parade of luxury cars headed from the cemetery, and we followed.

Rhoda looked more beautiful than I'd ever seen her. Although she'd been in tears she was moved by the respect that had been shown, and the beautiful flowers. And I hadn't let her down or embarrassed her. It was a big thing for her to be with a gorgia, and I knew she was worried about me being singled out or saying the wrong thing.

The pub was packed, three deep the length of the bar. Now that the official part of the day was done it was time to drink and reminisce. Lots of smiling faces recounting stories about the big man, arms beckoning fellow mourners to join in and add to the tales being told.

The conversations followed a pattern. We'd talk briefly about Riley, and they'd tell an anecdote about something he'd done, all escapades above the law. Needing to fit in at the wake, I chatted about living in a trailer with no water, no electricity, and getting hassle from the local council. I got lots of sympathy and advice, and I was slowly feeling part of the Traveller community.

The next hour was a mix of songs, some old favourites, and some that were new to me. Most of the crowd seemed to know them, and the choruses swelled with each pint consumed. It was a great atmosphere, and I thought how happy Riley would've been with his send-off. When numbers started thinning out we said our goodbyes and headed back to our caravan.

As we left the pub I had a chill down my spine. 'Someone's just walked over my grave,' I said to Rhoda.

'Come on,' she said. 'You're drunk.'

She took the wheel as I'd had a few pints, so I climbed into the passenger seat and off we drove. After half a mile a Transit van suddenly pulled in front of us. Rhoda had to slam on the brakes, throwing us forward in our seatbelts.

'Fucking idiot,' I gasped.

'What's happening?' shouted Rhoda. Another car stopped at an angle behind us, blocking us in.

As the men climbed out of the van I knew I was in trouble. Serious trouble.

The men stood there, three of them. Rough, hard Travelling men. One pointed at me through the windscreen, and another nodded.

'Meet me at the ford,' I told Rhoda, as they walked around to my door. 'I'll be there before sunset.' I had no idea where that statement came from, but I had to get Rhoda away and give her a place to rendezvous.

'What the hell are you saying?' she screamed. 'What's happening?'

'Just do it,' I said. 'I'll be there.'

Then I was yanked from the car, tangled in my seatbelt. 'Just leave the girl,' I shouted.

'Get in the fucking van, you bastard,' was all I heard.

I took some hard blows to the back of my head and shoulders as I climbed into the van. How had I been spotted? Who were these guys? Where the hell were they taking me?

Yet I felt strangely calm. For a long time I'd known this was coming. You can never really hope to escape the past. The door slammed shut behind me and I fell to the floor as the van pulled away. A series of well-aimed kicks and punches rained down as I tried to cover my head, rolling into a foetal position to protect myself. My head slammed back as I was kicked in the face, the pain of the other blows getting sharper.

Up to now I'd been passive, offering no resistance. Now I had to act or I was a dead man. I rolled on to my back as if to get away from another kick, bent my knees, and kicked out at the legs of the man in front of me. His knee snapped backwards. 'You bastard!' he screamed, as he crumpled.

I swung my head in time to miss a punch that would have finished me, scrambled to my feet and drove into the second guy. The driver craned his neck around, and shouted, 'Kill the fucker! Finish him! Knock him out!'

I rammed the second guy into the side of the van, and heard his teeth click together as his head struck the panel. Then I threw a hopeful uppercut with enough power to lift a horse. It connected. I felt his jaw break as I followed through, remembering my dad's advice: 'Aim an inch inside their head, son.' I aimed for two.

The van was slowing, the driver getting ready to climb through and help his friends. Thankfully the side door was unlocked so I slid it open and fell out, wincing at the pain in my ribs. The back of my head felt wet: blood was running down my neck.

Where was I? I didn't recognize the street but I started running, the bastards behind chasing. To live I had to run. To see Rhoda again I had to run. Breathing was agony – my ribs had to be broken. But I could run. Years of rugby had given me that skill, and now it was a live-or-die race.

Those guys were not athletes and I started to create some distance between us. Twenty yards became fifty and they pulled up to run back to their vehicles. Now I had to get off the road. Pacing myself across a couple of fields, I lost sight of the chasing vehicles. I paused to gather my breath, and my thoughts. My leather shoes were fucked, the suit trousers torn and now muddy to the knees. I had no phone – it was in the car with Rhoda. Had she got away? Was she safe?

I was knackered, but I had to keep moving. Every car engine I heard through the trees pushed me on. I knew roughly where I was now, and that ford was about four miles away. Sticking to hedgerows and copses, I made my way across country as the light faded. I was having to hold my lower ribs on the left side, the pain insufferable.

I stumbled on, the ground falling away now towards the tidal creek and the ford. Half a mile more and I could barely walk, let alone run. The water glistened as the sun dipped below the horizon. I knelt on the bank, almost too tired to raise my head.

After three hours of running and walking, I got to the ford at Alresford. And there sat Rhoda in her car. I was the opposite side of the channel but I could see she was furious. I had to cross the channel, lined with thick black mud. I stripped down to my boxers, holding my shoes in the air and leaving my trousers and shirt on the bank. The mud was cold, but the water was colder, salt stinging the cuts on my back and limbs.

Rhoda was already shouting as I climbed out. 'What the fucking hell did you do? You know they'll find you.'

Not *us*. Find *you* was all I heard and focused on.

'I was scared.' Her voice was brittle, raw. 'I went back to the pub for help and all they were talking about was you.'

I stood there, soaked and cold. Shaking with the reaction to both the freezing water and the emotions running through me.

'I'm sorry,' was all I could say.

'Sorry for threatening people with a gun? Or sorry for not telling me?'

She spoke in a strangely calm voice that sounded more ominous than if she'd shouted. And I had no answer. My brain was racing despite the last vestiges of any body heat draining through the soles of my feet and into the cold mud. The only time a gun had been involved was also the only time my face had been seen, so being recognized from the trip where the farmer had fired the shotgun made sense. But they hadn't connected the dots. Yet. Surely it was only a matter of time.

'It wasn't me with a gun,' I tried to explain, grasping at any chance to ease her anger. 'None of that was meant to happen. Things got out of hand.' I told her the story of how that day had unfolded. But I told it without any mention of the previous attacks, the petrol bombs.

But she knew.

'There was talk of caravans being burnt ten years ago.' Again, she spoke with that measured calm, looking me straight in the eye.

This was the moment. This was the exact second we'd never recover from. My shoulders went down as I exhaled a breath I hadn't realized I'd been holding. I could feel her slipping away as if it was a physical thing. Or as if someone was literally, as I stood there, cutting my heart out. This was everything I'd dreaded. All those friendly conversations at the wake would count for nothing once this story went round. And it would. The great pikey hunter fallen in love with one of their own. Living in a caravan on Gypsy land.

I felt sick. Sick with exhaustion, sick with fear. I could see the hard look on Rhoda's face, the rage, the temper.

29

We returned to the trailer, a nervous drive in silence. Rhoda was beyond angry – the fury in her face was clear to see. I had a range of emotions running through me, and now the adrenalin was starting to wear off, the shock set in. The realization of exactly what had happened, my past catching up with me, was a frightening prospect. We didn't know what to expect back at the plot, and I was fearing the worst. I half expected to find the blackened husk of our trailer smouldering, with my few possessions burnt to a crisp. Thankfully there was no tell-tale smudge of any smoke in the sky above the plot.

I got Rhoda to park on the roadside a distance from the caravan, and scouted ahead, tracking over the field and making sure no one was waiting for me at our home. I hardly noticed I was barefoot. My whole body was a mess of cuts, blood and mud, and as I crept through the bushes near the trailer I knew I had some injuries that needed attention. The gash on the back of my head had reopened and was bleeding again, and a dozen smaller cuts had been awakened by the cold salt water.

I crouched in the hedge, frozen to the bone in just my boxers, watching our caravan for movement. I counted as I watched, reaching two hundred. No sign of any unwanted company waiting for us. I slipped back to Rhoda and we drove to the gates. Now I knew that people had found me, and were after me, the caravan would always feel more like a fort to be defended than simply a home.

And still there was no conversation. Nothing I could say to Rhoda would've made any difference. After my time in Essex I'd changed my attitude towards Travelling folk: the only real help we'd received had been from members of Rhoda's community. But it didn't matter. What had happened today, what had happened all those years before, had set a clock ticking on our time in the caravan. On our time together.

It was a tense couple of weeks while I waited for my injuries to heal. The blow to my head needed stitches, but I made do without, nervous of visiting a hospital, having to explain my appearance and lie about the cause of my injuries. It was pretty obvious I'd been involved in a serious fight. My rugby experience assured me I'd cracked at least one rib, maybe more. Still, there was no treatment for that. It just made breathing difficult, and every position, whether sitting, lying down or simply walking, uncomfortable. Laughing would have been excruciating, but there was none of that going on. The smaller scuffs and cuts healed quickly, the worst being an inch-long gash on the sole of my left foot.

It was a sombre period. Riley was hardly cold and his family had started arguing and fighting. There were six daughters and countless cousins all split into factions. There was his land and other assets to argue over, and the family's collective grief was clouding the issue. Small comments blew up into huge quarrels, with everybody getting involved and trying to draw Rhoda into taking sides. The fighting wasn't helping her get any better, either. It was easy with all the recent events to forget that she was living with a serious illness, a condition that was a few tablets away from putting her back in hospital.

With everything that had happened it was best to steer clear of Rhoda's family, and to avoid anyone connected to Travellers. The threat of another Gypsy posse turning up at my caravan was constantly on my mind, and after a brief chat with Eddie I changed jobs. I was lucky enough to pick up some work for a guy doing insurance repairs, and had a job fixing a chalet near Portsmouth. Every morning I pulled away from the plot I was grateful that we'd had no unwanted visitors during the night, no rough hands dragging me out of bed and bundling me into the back of a van or, God forbid, waking us up with a petrol bomb exploding on the side of my own trailer. And I was paranoid enough on the daily drive to the south coast that I always kept an eye on who was behind me, often making random turns and taking diversions if someone stayed on my tail for more than a few miles.

Just my luck that the chalet was owned by some Gypsy folk. It was one of half a dozen spread around some land belonging to a large house they'd bought. My initial nerves when driving between the stone horses' heads mounted on the gate pillars, the typical emblem of a Traveller homestead, faded as I realized there was no way these people would know me. Surely not. The job was a blatant scam: they'd gone round the chalet with a watering can after a tiny leak in the bathroom. They'd declared the damage was throughout the chalet, resulting in a claim for new floors, carpets and furniture. But I was there to do the work, not pass judgement, and they were nice enough to me, not knowing who I was and what I'd done to their brethren in the past.

It was a long, boring journey around London to Portsmouth, and the radio in the Land Rover wasn't working so offered no relief. Relief from the thoughts about the mess I'd made of my life, about what was going to happen to my relationship with Rhoda. I needed a distraction for the long drive, and remembered that during the summer her grandfather had given her an old white carrier bag full of cassette tapes. He'd often visited us on his own, and hardly ever without giving her a present. Tapes were more or less obsolete, and the bag had been dumped in the shed and forgotten. But my old Land Rover had a tape player that might still work, and it was on the Sunday while I was loading the Land Rover with tools that I found the carrier bag again.

'Would you mind if I took that bag of tapes with me?' I asked Rhoda.

She nodded okay, so I put the bag in the front seat. We were at least communicating again, but it was only polite small-talk. I'd tried to explain that all of the troubles were from years before but she'd waved me away, not prepared to listen. I felt like I'd lost her, and it was breaking my heart. Stoically carrying on, doing the everyday things without being able to talk to each other about the most important thing in our lives, was devastating.

I got up at dawn the next morning and started the Land Rover, the familiar engine roar sending birds scattering. There was a chill in the air as I got out to relock the gates after driving onto the road. The constant locking and unlocking was a chore but had become a necessity. Pulling away I reached into the carrier bag on the passenger seat. The tapes were numbered one to twelve, and I put in the first expecting to hear some Gypsy folk music. There was a silence of about thirty seconds, and I was starting to think the tapes were blank or spoilt by time. Then Riley's voice came over the speakers: 'My name is Riley, a Travelling man from Tiptree in Essex, and this is my life story.'

I immediately pulled over and called Rhoda to let her hear a few minutes of her grandfather. I was holding my phone to the speakers. She was crying. 'That's my granddad,' I heard her say to herself a few times. I could hear the love through the tears, the comfort of hearing his voice once again.

On my journeys back and forth to Portsmouth I listened to all of those tapes, the life that Riley had led. He started with his earliest memories of going to Ireland, aged five or six, with his grandfather, who had visited every year to buy horses and carts, ponies and traps, and ship it all back to England. The strange-looking herd and collection of carts would fill the ferry completely, both levels. Riley would spend his days helping his grandfather keep the animals moving, and at night he slept under a blanket on a bale of hay they carried for fodder. Travelling back from Liverpool to their home in Tiptree they'd sell most of the stock on the way. His grandfather taught him tricks to help sell a lame horse, such as sending him to the nearest hedgerow to cut a piece of blackthorn. This would be whittled into a fierce splinter, which was then pushed into the good hoof so the animal couldn't favour either leg and lost the appearance of lameness.

If a horse got canker of the hoof his grandfather would gouge out the rot and pack the infected hoof with a mix of tar and sawdust. After walking it round the yard for a while, muck and dust would stick to the tar making the hoof look and smell normal. The horse would probably be dead within a week, but they'd be long gone by then.

Riley went on to talk of meeting his lifelong love, Tillie, whom he married and with whom he'd had six daughters, one, of course, being Rhoda's mother. He'd seen Tillie in a different camp from his own, and feeling that her family were above his, he'd been scared to ask her father for permission to go walking with her. But she was as keen on him as he was on her, and the young couple ran off to a third camp to spend the night. Although they were chaperoned by trusted elders, Tillie's father was furious when they returned the next morning, but grudgingly gave his blessing to the union.

I couldn't imagine how it must have been living on

the road raising six daughters. Throughout the tapes Riley would simply mention the arrival of another baby, each one being one of Rhoda's aunts, whom I'd met in person. Riley had a smile in his voice recalling how he'd caught Rhoda's mother in a cupboard mixing flour and butter into her hair. He'd chased her round and round but she kept ducking under the caravan.

His life was one of hard graft, and even with a young family he'd travelled around following seasonal work. As I said earlier, farmers had depended on this labour force. Jobs such as hop picking in Kent, topping off acres of turnips, were all done by Travellers for grateful farmers. It was the mechanization of farming that had destroyed the relationship. And nothing had filled the void left in the community's lifestyle. Suddenly they were no longer required, no longer welcome. In the space of two generations they'd gone from essential helpers to unwelcome guests, and it seemed the farmers had short memories. I listened to Riley narrate the passing of that time, of the pain it caused when the farmers turned their backs. It made me feel sick to remember my small part in that ongoing battle. Through my lack of understanding and sympathy with their lifestyle and history, I'd added to their troubles.

With nothing put in place to give the travellers an income, they were forced to get by however they could. Riley spoke openly about the various prisons he'd served time in. One of my favourite stories involved him being on a work detail tidying a local graveyard at the vicar's request. The prison officer supervising was having an affair with a lady living down the road and would leave the prisoners alone for hours at a time. Riley arranged with his wife to have bottles of whisky and roast chickens hidden in the graveyard. After a short spell of work, he and his companions would sit in the sunshine enjoying the food and drink. It reminded me of that rooftop scene in *The Shawshank Redemption*, when the prisoners are rewarded for their labours with a bottle of cold beer.

Riley also told a story of getting stuck in snow in Kent on a country lane for nearly two weeks, melting snow for water and shooting pheasants to eat. When eventually a snowplough came down the road Riley pulled out behind him and followed him to the county border. The driver had wanted to turn back but Riley insisted he carried on to the main road so he and Tillie could push on with their journey. Bearing in mind Riley's size and powers of persuasion, it was no surprise the chap pressed on into the next county.

Most of Riley's tales involved a fight, either being part of one or discussing one he'd witnessed. It amused me when he claimed he had never started a fight but had finished many. Having met the man in his later years, I could still clearly see the strength in his shoulders, arms and hands. I wouldn't have chosen to confront him even then.

While Riley was away it fell to Tillie to keep the family together and earn an income. And Tillie was no less fearsome than her husband. Firewood was a constant sideline, and Riley told of how Tillie could swing an eight-pound splitting axe as hard as any man and for twice as long. A chap had come to their yard to start work splitting logs and Tillie had sacked him when he'd walked just ten yards towards her. When Riley asked her why, she said he'd climbed over some firewood like a sissy. 'No chance he could do a proper day's work.'

There was no hiding that life was hard, but I also understood the sense of freedom Riley had achieved. A sense of living under his own rules. I could see the appeal. Riley's stories came from a time in history when the whole Gypsy community had been rejected, when society had chosen to turn its back on them. His early tales of helping farmers with their crops held humour and warmth. Gypsies had been recycling long before it was government policy, for years collecting scrap metal and unwanted clothes for the rag trade. When Riley spoke, you could hear his dignity, his pride in his family and his heritage, and his freedom.

In the weeks after Riley passed away the arguments rumbled on between the family over who should have what. But Rhoda had the greatest inheritance of all beyond money. Having her grandfather's life recorded in such a way was priceless, a wonderful tale of Gypsy culture, told in vivid detail by a true Gypsy legend.

Despite the joy that her grandfather's tapes had brought to her, Rhoda and I had hardly had a proper conversation since the funeral. The atmosphere between us was terrible. When you're living in a caravan it's very difficult to give each other any space, and Rhoda had taken to spending long hours lying on her bed. I knew that every day, every hour that passed, I was closer to losing her. But I had no answers.

'Fancy taking Alfie out?' I asked, hoping a walk might give us a chance to talk.

'I'm not feeling right,' she replied, avoiding eye contact.

So I went out for a walk with just Alfie for company. It was still warm weather, but the leaves were starting to turn, glowing red and bronze on the sunny day. There was an odd bridge over the main road about a mile away across the fields, built when the road had been made, years ago, but no car had ever driven over it. I crossed it and followed Alfie, field after field, the hedgerows occasionally exploding with disturbed pheasants. Then the light began to fade, and I realized I'd been gone for most of the afternoon. By the time I got back it was almost dark.

The plot was quiet as I approached, and Rhoda hadn't yet started the generator.

I poked my head inside. 'Do you want me to start the generator?'

She was standing in the middle of the trailer, arms crossed, and silent. All around her were bags and boxes.

'What's going on?' I asked, even though I knew the answer. 'What are all the bags about?'

She was leaving. I struggled to say it out loud in case that made it true. After losing so much, I didn't think I could cope with any more.

'I'm going to stay at my aunt's house for a while,' she tried to explain. 'Living here isn't helping my condition.'

She spoke quietly, but firmly. I knew the real reason she was leaving. We both did. But her excuse held enough truth for both of us to put a front on things, to avoid the shattering reality.

'Okay,' I replied. 'I understand. Is there anything I can do to help?'

Inside I was breaking apart. Any moment now I was going to be physically sick.

'The generator,' Rhoda said gently. 'It's pretty dark in here.'

She looked stunning. Despite being upset she was still so beautiful in that tragic moment.

I went outside and kicked the generator over. A cloud of noxious fumes sent me back out of the woodshed. I stood and stared through the window, brightly lit from the inside compared to the dusk outside. We stood there gazing at each other, the noise of the generator seeming to fade as time stood still. I reached my hand up and placed it on the glass. Rhoda mirrored my hand from the inside, our flesh separated only by the cool windowpane. The glass seemed to represent the fragile moment, how close everything was to shattering around us. She closed her eyes, turning slowly, her hand leaving mine alone on the window. I turned away and wandered down the plot to gather my thoughts. What on earth was I going to do now? I was losing my girlfriend, and possibly my second home within a year. Would Tony let me stay here on my own, without his daughter?

I could feel all the stress crowding my head, and there were no easy answers. I was clinging to the hope that this was only a short-term thing, but the huge pile of Rhoda's bags spoke volumes. It was over. My past had ruined my future, and there was nothing I could do. After half an hour of thinking about everything, but not achieving a single coherent thought, I walked back up to the trailer.

'How are you getting there?' I asked. 'I can fit this lot in the Land Rover easy enough.'

Rhoda had obviously expected a different reaction. 'Thank you.' She smiled, a half-smile, and it was like a knife in my guts. I kept the emotion off my face and started moving bags and boxes out of the caravan into the Land Rover. Within ten minutes we were driving into Colchester.

'What will you do?' she finally asked.

'No idea,' I replied. 'I'm kind of stuck now.'

'I've spoken to Dad,' she said. 'You can stay there as long as you need to.'

Her words were intended to be kind and helpful, but they just confirmed that we were over. The finality of it was hard to bear. I felt truly lost and alone.

I knew just how precarious my situation was now. I had no options, my money was all gone, and I had debts to repay, a life to rebuild. I couldn't think straight. The next hour seemed like a bad dream, unloading her things into her aunt's house, and the stony silence from everyone there, before a brief hug goodbye. Was this actually the end? Was I now alone? Again, I was asking myself, how on earth had it come to this?

I drove back to the trailer, let Alfie out for a run, and opened a bottle of beer. I lit the wood-burner and settled on the couch with Alfie's head on my lap. Only the crackle of the fire broke the silence, and its light the darkness. The thought of unwanted visitors was now a constant stress on my mind. But I had to drop those thoughts, get positive. I tried to remember one of my favourite quotes from Churchill: 'If you're going through hell, keep going.'

If I just rolled over and gave up it would be the end. I would rebuild, I told myself. I would come back from this.

30

For a few weeks I could do nothing except walk the dog and drink beer. I'd got myself into a routine of just getting through the days, each one a trial, from waking up to crashing out on the couch. The beer helped take the edge off my anxiety as I was constantly on edge, a marked man, alone. And while the alcohol allowed me to sleep, my diet consisted of what the local chip shop could provide. I was comfort-eating doner kebab and southern fried chicken, sometimes both in the same meal.

I was waiting for a visit to the plot, constantly looking out of my window, waking up at the slightest sound. The guys from the funeral must have asked around for where I was living. I couldn't understand why they hadn't been over to have another go at me. If they did, I was ready. I'd stashed makeshift weapons around the caravan, and I was always within a few yards of anything from an air rifle to a baseball bat to an axe. Thank God for Alfie, my natural guard dog, permanently on alert, listening for the approach of any unwanted arrivals. But I was running out of nerve, money and options.

It was a phone call from my cousin Stephen that kicked me back into life. There was a chance of some work nearby: a tidal creek had surged and wiped out some static homes on a park near Bentley, just down the coast. It was an insurance job, installing a flood wall the length of the park to steer the next tidal surge over the opposite bank into meadows rather than the park. Stephen met me down there and introduced me to the contractor. We shook hands and agreed I would start the next day. That night I was glad to go to bed with a sense of purpose.

This was the start of a better time, a recovery of sorts, with money coming in while I was working on a beautiful tidal creek on the Essex coast. The work was physically hard, but exactly what I needed. At the end of the shift, if the tide was in, I would go for a swim in the estuary: having no water at home meant this was the best option for keeping myself clean.

The folk who ran the park were nice enough to us but terrible to the residents who lived there. Trailer parks were springing up all over the place, yet another example of us following America's lead with no real thought of the consequences. Decades before, folk had been housed in council accommodation, large three- or four-bedroom houses built to the highest standard. Now they'd been sold off and poorer families were ending up in these caravans. Vulnerable people, who'd fallen on tough times, were trapped in one-sided contracts and treated like crap. An old Gypsy worked there, and he knew Riley and Tillie from years before. Once I got to know him a bit better, and trusted that he wouldn't go snitching on who I was and where I was working, I told him my connection to the family and how I was living in a caravan up the road.

'What are you running that Land Rover on?' he asked one day.

'Diesel,' I answered, not really understanding the point of the question.

'Come up to the workshop on the way out,' he offered. 'I'll fill your tank with red.'

Now I knew what he meant. Most Travellers run their vans and trucks on red diesel, a heavily subsidized fuel that's dyed red and only permitted for use in licensed agricultural vehicles. I told the old Gypsy I was always scared of being dipped by the DVSA and getting fined. He laughed like a drain and said the Old Bill never pulled over Land Rovers because most were driven by farmers. He took me up to the workshop area where they had the diesel tank for the plant on site. Within ten minutes I had a full tank, and instead of the usual eighty quid on a garage forecourt I handed over a twenty and we were both happy.

As I'd been taken more and more into the confidence of the various Travellers I was mixing with they'd laughed about how they changed the letters on the backs of their cars to avoid being pulled over for fuel tests. Instead of 'TDI', the acronym for Turbocharged Direct Injection, an engine design specific to diesel, they'd fox the police by sticking on the petrol equivalent '24v' and rarely got pulled over. Simple but, according to the lads, it worked a treat as the authorities ignored what they thought were petrol cars.

I ended up spending a good year working on that wall,

through a warm summer and a bitterly cold winter. Frozen coastal clay has to be the hardest material known to man to dig by hand, but I stuck at it, and I was genuinely sad when the job came to an end. It had done me good by forcing me to cut down on my boozing, and eat proper food. I'd even started to relax in the caravan without drinking myself into a stupor. I was feeling healthy enough, mentally and physically, to start playing rugby again, and had been turning out for Colchester. They ran a social side made up of veterans and some young lads, and I loved the escape of getting back into the game. There is a special bond in the rugby family that goes beyond class or origin, and the boys from Colchester were a great example of that. I was made welcome and it was a massive lift when I needed it most.

Although the end of the work on the tidal wall had left me jobless again, I spotted a post on Facebook for a welder and left a comment that I was interested. A few days later I got a reply and, as luck would have it, an opposition rugby player worked there and had recognized my face. I got the job. Once again, my rugby family had given me a hand in life when I most needed it.

I was now working for a small engineering firm based in Brightlingsea. There were only four of us, three on the tools, and the guv'nor, Keith. It was Keith's combination of cheerful bluster and can-do attitude that kept the firm so busy. But it was the lads on the tools who made it such a success. I loved my time there. Getting my hands back on the business end of a welder felt right.

The work we did varied from fairly heavy steel work on building sites to decorative balconies and stairwell balustrades. We even repaired some mobile targets on the local gun range at Colchester barracks. Over the years the one thing I'd learnt was that in engineering you never stop acquiring new skills, and that was true of my time in Brightlingsea.

It was ideal for collecting water, too. The stand pipe I used was right there so I could go straight over after work and fill up the jerry cans. It was strange how, after a while, I became immune to the judgemental stares from local dog-walkers. I often went there at the same time after leaving work, and as we're all creatures of habit I'd frequently see the same people and their dogs. After seeing me a number of times they'd guess I was collecting free water for use at home. I was embarrassed the first few times I saw the scorn on their faces, but my shame soon passed. To some of the more dour folk I deliberately called out a cheery greeting, forcing them to say hello to someone they'd probably decided was a water-thieving vagrant.

They'd shut off the dog tap in the colder months of winter in fear of the pipes bursting, and I'd been getting my water from the cemetery in Colchester. The tap there was for folk putting flowers on graves or cleaning headstones. It was a lagged standpipe so was on all year, and I just had to get there before the gates were locked. On a few occasions I was late and had to jump over the wall with a single container, desperate enough for water to risk getting caught.

My fears and concerns over leaving the plot all day, leaving Alfie to fend for himself, had faded as I got stuck into work that I was enjoying. I was settling into a routine, working hard, fetching water, and still calling in to the caravan park for some cheap diesel. Then, suddenly, something changed. The old Gypsy wasn't as friendly, and hinted that our arrangement was over. I asked him if I'd said anything wrong, but he just dropped his head, not meeting my eyes.

My heart sank. Was the past catching up again? I shook his hand and said goodbye, and that was the last I saw of him.

31

From the moment I'd arrived at the plot in Elmstead Market I'd caught the attention of both the parish council and the local council based in Tendring. Parish councillors are basically nosy bastards with too much time on their hands. Under the flimsy pretence of public service they enjoy a self-assumed right to poke their beaks into other folk's business, expressing unsolicited and unwelcome opinions on everything from the colour of your front door to what time you have a shit in the morning. With no actual powers, they hold meetings about scheduling more meetings, which are basically a chance to gossip and be negative about the community they're meant to serve. They'd probably been bullied at school. Elmstead Market was no different. Sitting in a planning meeting listening to their tripe was like having teeth pulled. But I did it with a smile, successfully schmoozing the jobsworths by making all the right noises, winning their full support for my planning application. I think they were so relieved to find out I wasn't a bona fide Traveller that they'd have supported anything I proposed.

I had no issues from the neighbours. As it was a care home the staff didn't mind my presence either way, and the poor residents were unable to form a single coherent word, let alone express an opinion. So that left Tendring District Council.

I made visit after visit to their office in Weeley, and each time I left more confused and disheartened. Misinformation from the start, completing the wrong forms, wasting my time and theirs. From the beginning it had been clear that I'd struggle to get a change-of-use permission for the plot. It had been untouched for forty years, left to become the overgrown patch of waste ground I'd originally cleared. There was a pavement, albeit sunken, so roadside access was established, and it was well within the village envelope for buildings. But the brick wall I was running into on every visit was bureaucracy.

Without a change of use I couldn't get a postal address. Without an address I couldn't get any services connected. So I was still living with no water or electricity.

'You'll never get planning on that plot.'

I was talking to an elderly guy from the village outside the shop.

'Why not?' I wondered. 'I'm doing everything they ask me to.'

'It's Gypsy land. The council got burnt with Dale Farm, and they won't let it happen again.'

Dale Farm had been Europe's largest Traveller camp. Established just outside Basildon in the 1970s when a group of Romany families had settled on land beside a scrapyard, all had gone relatively well until the 1990s when Irish Travellers had bought the site. The plot virtually doubled, the population rapidly grew, and the legal battle with the local government began.

Oddly enough that battle for land, fought on one side by local residents in the next-door village of Crays Hill, and on the other by dozens of Traveller families, from great-grandkids to great-grandparents, had developed over the same period during which my own feelings towards Gypsies had dramatically shifted. When Dale Farm first hit the headlines at the start of the new millennium I was planning rides out in the middle of the night to burn caravans. Ten years later, when a government-sanctioned mob of bailiffs and coppers finally moved in to haul the Travellers out, I was in love with Rhoda and fully aware of what strife this enforced eviction would bring to the folk in caravans and trailers.

Some of the Dale Farm residents had been brought up on the road in a traditional wagon, and I knew from talking to Riley and Tillie how hard that life had been. Now, after years of living in one place, with a fresh-water supply and electricity mains – the plots at Dale Farm were fully connected to mains power and water, unlike my own little site – along with opportunities for the children to attend the local school regularly, they were reduced to a precarious lifestyle of driving from one site to another, hoping to find patches of land to camp far enough away from angry locals, people like my friend the farmer and, if they were lucky enough, people like me. Or at least the person I'd once been, the rash young man with a bellyful of beer and drunken promises to chase the Gypsies away for a few quid in my pocket.

Anyway, the media loved the Dale Farm story. Journalists reported on the Travellers making their case for a right to live on the land, as well as the insistence by the local council, and the residents affected by the site, that they had to move. And I was in the position of understanding both points of view.

One particular name, Len Grindley, popped up over and over again in that sad story. Sick of the travellers coming onto his property that adjoined the site, stealing whatever wasn't nailed down or simply making a mess by dumping their rubbish in his back garden, he'd erected an eight-foot-high steel fence and invited camera crews into his house to see the mess. No surprise he attracted the ire of his neighbours. At a televised public meeting at Basildon Town Hall, when the councillors formally voted to evict the Travellers from Dale Farm, one of the women shouted across the room that they'd kill him. A very public death threat. Well, I could sympathize with him there. I could also sympathize with the folk in the trailers just trying to find a little corner of this country to be left alone.

When I heard that Len had been the default leader of his local community, organizing meetings with affected residents, and even paying for helicopter flyovers with his own money to photograph and monitor the site and its development, I had to compare his efforts to mine back in Ledburgh. I'd been the one to step up and take on the Smiths. I'd been the one who had done the dirty work for farmers too afraid to take on the Travellers themselves. It had all seemed so black and white back then. Here were people living illegally, a blight on good folk paying their taxes and abiding by the law. I was fronting up when others weren't, being the hero, if I'm honest, and perhaps Len felt just as righteous about his actions. But then he hadn't fallen in love with a beautiful Romany woman and traded in his house for a caravan.

Although the Dale Farm eviction motion had been agreed by councillors in 2005, it wasn't until six years later, and after numerous appeals and protests, including legal help from non-Gypsy activists across the globe, that the order was executed.

An estimated four hundred Travellers were living there illegally by the time of the widely publicized evictions in 2011. It was a brutal stand-off, with the Travellers claiming they had nowhere to go, and the local council insisting that the law be upheld. The case had ultimately gone all the way to the House of Lords, culminating in an army of bailiffs and police using heavy plant to clear the site. The bill was in excess of six million pounds, and the media had a field day. I remember watching the evictions live on the news. Huge yellow JCBs shunting through barricades thrown up by activists and the residents, the latter trying to protect their homes. Bricks and bottles were thrown – one bloke was even tased. Countless bailiffs decked in hi-vis jackets used sledge-hammers to demolish fences and walls, while policemen handcuffed men, women and children, as the great government machinery crushed their caravans.

My plot wouldn't have been anything remotely like that, but the experience had shaped local authorities' opinions on any Travellers or Gypsies setting up camp on any land, whether they owned it or not.

Therefore feelings, just as the old man outside the shop had rightly pointed out, were running high in the local area about another potential site springing up. I'd never been a victim of prejudice before I'd started living in a trailer, like a Gypsy. Jesus, in the eyes of the council I *was* a Gypsy. Even though I'd stated that the plot was intended for single occupancy they hadn't believed me. If I'd got planning permission I'd have been able to pull as many caravans onto there as would fit, and that was what frightened them. Another rag-tag convoy of trailers and trucks camped on the edge of the village.

So, the endless process I'd begun was without conclusion – except their deliberate policy of denial. The final reason for my rejection was adjudicated by some walking clipboard from Bristol, working for the Highways Agency. He rejected the application based on concerns regarding access. He'd visited the site when I was away and refused to come back to discuss it again. Decision made. What a prick.

There I was, living in a caravan with no services, no chance of planning, and a time limit set on my being there. And why? Because the land was owned by a Gypsy, and in turn I was assumed to be a Gypsy.

My reactions ranged from outrage and frustration to laughing at the irony. I was now a direct victim of the very discrimination I'd so enthusiastically expressed ten years before. Talk about karma. It was a hopeless situation.

32

Mentally, this period was a real challenge for me. The council had told me I was officially homeless, and I was starting to feel more and more vulnerable on the plot. Despite work going well, I was feeling more and more certain that I was going to get a visit to my caravan, and that my past was coming full circle. The violence I'd meted out all those years ago was finally returning to its origins. My only company was Alfie. The bond between man and dog had never been stronger, and it was his boundless joy for life that kept me going.

I had phone calls with my parents but I'd never felt able to describe the muddle I'd got myself into. Years before, my father had warned me about Sam and my business: he'd seen something in him that I'd missed. But I'd considered him my friend and continued to trust him. So the situation was of my own making, and even now, at my most desperate point, my stubborn pride wouldn't allow me to ask for help. My oldest friend had called me once since the funeral, and as I described living with no water, he'd made all kinds of promises to help. I never heard from him again. They say a friend in need is a pain in the arse, and so it seemed. So, my loyal hound, Alfie, was my salvation.

I was still working for Keith, and some of our days were long, fitting steel work into sites in Cambridge. Alfie was left at the plot, shut into the trailer while I was at work, and his enthusiastic welcome on my return, leaping up and licking my face, tail wagging and his happy bark when I got out of the Land Rover, was incredibly consoling.

I was cutting the grass one evening when one of the staff from the care home came up to the fence. I went over to say hello, as the staff there had always been friendly and supported my efforts to stay on the plot.

'How's things going?' I asked, wiping the fresh-cut grass off my boots.

'Oh, same old as always,' she replied, cordially enough, but I sensed something else in her tone. 'You had some visitors today,' she continued. 'Three men. Looked a bit dodgy.'

The news made my world stand still, and my stomach churned. 'What – just wandering around the plot?'

She went on to explain that they'd just walked off when she'd called out to them.

'They must have climbed over the gate,' I told her. 'It's always locked.'

I thanked her for keeping an eye out for me, and went back to the mower. This was the worst thing I could have heard. There were two possibilities, both as bad as each other. If those guys had been chancers, all my things would disappear over the next few days and weeks. They'd soon realize I was out during the day and could just take what they wanted. The generator, all my tools, everything in both the container and the caravan was up for grabs. Including Alfie. I felt sick at the thought of him being used as training bait for some Traveller's dog fights.

The second possibility was that I'd been found again. And they'd come in numbers, which was a cause for serious worry. I wandered around the plot, rechecking my makeshift weapons caches. If it came to a scrap in the open I had a few surprises lined up. But this was crazy thinking. If they came prepared I was pretty much fucked. You could combine all the Bruce Lee shit with a truckload of luck, but in the real world I was in a bugger's muddle, and I knew it. I had a restless night hanging onto the air rifle with a table across the door. It wasn't the first night's sleep I'd had in that position, and it certainly wasn't the last.

Then three days later, on a pitch-black evening, Alfie went crazy outside. He's a German Pointer, so actually a great big softie of a dog, but his bark is that of a ten-stone Rottweiler. And he really was barking, running back and forth, getting more and more agitated. I still had my army boots on so jumped up and grabbed my baseball bat, a favourite weapon that I'd bought in Manhattan and always kept leaning against the door frame. When I took hold of it, I drew comfort from the feel of it in my hand.

Until I walked round the trailer and my worst fears were realized.

It was a black night, but I could see the sidelights of a

van parked in front of the gates. Three men were standing there, my loyal Alfie's snarl keeping them from coming over the rail. He'd never have bitten anyone, but they didn't know that.

I walked to the gates, heart pumping, adrenalin surging through my body. Yet I was strangely calm, as if I'd accepted what was inevitable.

'What do you want?' I called across the gate, my voice raised above Alfie's barking. 'It's a bit late for a social visit.'

'Who are ya?' One of them answered my question with his own.

'Jerry Thompson,' I lied, no idea where the name had come from.

I was standing there in my army boots, cargo shorts and a rugby shirt, with a baseball bat in my hand. It was obvious I wasn't there for small-talk.

'We need a place to pull in for a few nights,' said a different man.

Now we were talking Alfie had gone quiet, but he was standing behind me. That was unusual: once greetings were voiced he'd normally bounce over to say hello. Not this time. He'd picked up on the tension, and was waiting for the fight to begin.

'Fuck off,' I replied. 'You're not coming in here.' I sounded much calmer than I felt. My left knee was shaking so badly surely they had to see it. I moved my feet in an effort to steady my leg.

'Why not? You're a Traveller, and we only need a spot

for two nights.' The first guy was talking again. 'What family are you part of?'

'Never you mind about my family,' I snapped. 'You're not coming in here. First one over that gate gets a broken head.'

I raised the bat. A man put his hand on the gate and I swung the bat down, clattering the rail. He flinched and whipped his arm back as the contact cracked through the night. I'd missed him by an inch.

'You stupid bastard,' he shouted, and for the first time I heard the unmistakable Irish lilt to his voice.

'I warned you fuckers,' I shouted. 'I'll break your fucking arm next time.'

Alfie was barking again, adding to the noise.

It was an impasse. I couldn't, and didn't want to, go over the gate. They couldn't get over without risking a crack from the bat. We stood and stared at each other.

'Just fuck off and don't come back,' I bellowed.

Finally they turned and walked towards their van. 'We'll be back, you bastard,' one said, full of menace.

I stood in the dark as their lights arced round with the van backing onto the road. White Transit, what a surprise. They revved away, leaving silence behind. Alfie was mouthing my wrist, as if needing reassurance that he'd done okay. I dropped to my knees and hugged him, taking the licks, squeezing him close to me. There was no way I'd have got through that without him. But what to do now?

I went back into the trailer. My mind was racing, and

I was fearing the worst. How was I going to be safe tonight? There was no way I could sleep in the caravan. I was more at risk inside than out. And I knew full well how they burnt.

I parked the Land Rover with the back facing the gates at a distance of about thirty yards. I made up a bed-roll and space for Alfie, then propped open the rear door with a piece of timber. My alarm system was that if anyone came near the plot Alfie would hear them and jump out barking. I could then follow with the air rifle. It was crazy, but it was a plan. With the warm body of the dog against my legs, the rifle and baseball bat within easy reach, I went to sleep. And I slept pretty well considering the circumstances.

Next morning I woke early, at first light. Alfie was sitting up straight, but still beside me. 'Go on, boy,' I said. 'Out you go.' I patted him on the back, my trusty guard dog, and he leapt out. He set off on his usual round of scaring pigeons and pissing on the perimeter of the plot, marking his territory. I watched him, graceful and sure-footed, the drama of last night seemingly forgotten.

As Alfie bounded around the trailer, I knew I had to leave. I was living on borrowed time. If they didn't get me, they might harm my dog, and I couldn't bear the thought of that. I owed him too much. Leaving him here while I was at work all day was a huge risk now.

He came trotting back to the Land Rover. 'What are we going to do now, Alfie?' I was rubbing his ears, making a real fuss of him.

He looked at me, his solid, loyal gaze, eye to eye, a total bond.

'Time to move on,' I admitted to him. 'Time to rebuild. Let's get packing.'

As I started packing my life into the Land Rover and my box trailer, I couldn't help but see how wrong I'd been all those years ago. Most of the Gypsies I'd met had offered me help and advice. The people I'd expected help from had stayed away.

Before I finished packing I called Rhoda and told her I was leaving the caravan. I chose not to mention last night's visit to the plot. She soon arrived and pulled her car in beside the Land Rover. The trailer was almost fully loaded.

Rhoda got out of her car, first making a fuss of Alfie, who was bustling round her legs, pleased to see her. As was I – she looked as gorgeous as ever. Knowing the effort that went into creating that seemingly effortless beauty always made me smile. Yet my feelings had changed, and although I'd lost the daydream of romance with Rhoda, the happy memories of us together would always remain.

'What made you decide to move on?' she asked. 'You know Dad said you could stay here as long as you needed to.'

'It just feels like the right time,' I said, truthfully enough. 'I'm in a rut here and I need to get back into my world. I need to start living a normal life again. Maybe even have a bath.' I laughed, trying to ease the tension.

'Okay.' She shrugged. 'Well, you know where I am if you need anything.'

We hugged, not the emotionally charged hug we'd shared after the separation – the weeks and months had eased that pain – but the hug of two people who had accepted that some things were out of their control.

And there I was, loading up my life again and hitching the trailer. I opened the gate for the last time. Alfie jumped onto the seat beside me, his tail wagging, sensing a new adventure. I pulled through the gates and, in the mirror, watched Rhoda close them behind me, fitting a new lock of her own, another symbol of our end. Briefly she held up her hand as a goodbye, then turned to walk back down the plot.

I pulled forward to the edge of the road with no definite plans or destination. Should I turn left or right?

August 2018

When I hit the light switch, the light comes on. I twist the tap and water flows into the sink: running water, when I need it, without having to drive down to the dog tap in Brightlingsea and fill my car with jerry cans. The central heating kicks in with the thermostat, and I wake up warm and content. Two years on from hitching up my trailer and hitting the road, I have a home. Not quite bricks and mortar but it's my home. And I still have my Alfie.

The day I left the plot behind I felt a strange sense of separation. Despite having no home, I felt my time living as a Traveller was coming to an end. I knew that my future would be hard in the short term, and I was effectively having to rebuild from nothing. But I had faith and confidence that I could reclaim a place in normal society.

That I could go on.

After the beating from the Gypsies, then watching Rhoda walk out of the door, a caravan door at that, I'd been living through a very dark time. Feeling luckless and isolated, I'd struggled with depression. I remember one occasion when I walked Alfie across the fields to the bridge over the main road. On that day I'd been drinking heavily. Drink only ever emphasizes your state of mind, your mood, and I was unhappy and lonely. I'd arrived on the bridge in a daze, walking automatically, thinking of everything yet thinking of nothing. I knew I'd reached my limit for living as I was. Did I consider climbing over the handrail and ending it? Did I consider the pain of landing on the road below, of the impact of a forty-foot lorry? Yes, I did. I stood there with my hands on the rail. Then I felt something push against me. Alfie. Pushing himself between me and the barrier. Looking me in the eye. How long had I been there? I have no idea. And were Alfie's actions caused by a simple impatience to get moving, or had he sensed my mood? Either way he broke the spell. He brought me back to reality. That moment has stayed with me and still pushes me forwards to live a full and successful life.

After driving away from the plot I needed a break. And, thank my lucky stars, I got one. A good friend called me out of the blue with a proposition. He had access to a lake where the owner was experiencing difficulties with unwanted visitors. Nothing too heavy, just groups of kids swimming, having campfires and smoking weed by the shore. It had stopped him visiting his own property through an aversion to confrontation. He needed someone to stay there and look after the place.

On the site there was a beautiful wooden lodge overlooking the lake, which would be available for me to live in. It ticked every box. Isolated, space for Alfie, and hard to find for any vengeful Gypsies. Within a couple of weeks I was happily setting up home in the lodge and enjoying the lake. It had been stocked with fish ten years before and had never seen a rod. There were huge carp, tench and rudd drifting between patches of lily-pads. The whole place was surrounded by forest, and in the early mornings I'd regularly see different breeds of deer drinking from the lake. Buzzards would catch a thermal and rise ever higher into clear blue skies.

In return for this refuge all I had to do was some minor maintenance to the cabin and some general tidying up around the property. It was pure therapy from the stress of the caravan, of feeling like a marked man. It remains one of the happiest periods of my life. All of my troubles, losing my business, losing my home, seemed to fade. It gave me time to get over the loss of Rhoda and our time together.

Alfie loved to swim, endlessly trying to catch fish that seemed to tease him before diving just out of reach. I'd spend hours in the water with him, drifting lazily as he swam in circles around me. There was barely a phone signal in the area, so the feeling of isolation was intense. At first this was coupled with anxiety and the thought that I'd be completely on my own if anyone did track me down. But as the peace of the lake took hold the anxiety faded, and was finally replaced with a contentment I'd forgotten was even possible.

During my time there I had only a few visitors, and simply parking my vehicle was enough to keep most folk away. Occasionally harmless ramblers, or kids looking for a quick swim, passed by.

Late one night a car pulled up outside the cabin, and the driver left the engine running. I woke up and checked the time. It was almost midnight. Once again my heart started thumping, the paranoia kicking in that I'd been found again. Heavy footsteps scuffed along the decking that surrounded the building, and I swiftly grabbed a heavy Maglite torch with my trusty baseball bat and headed for the door. Alfie was already up, his body vibrating with tension. I whipped open the door to the pitch black outside, and Alfie erupted onto the decking, his snarling bark flaring wildfowl into the air to amplify the explosion of noise. I followed Alfie round the side of the cabin and turned on the torch. Alfie was running round and round the invading car, barking and growling, while two pairs of legs poked out of the front windows, clearly stuck.

Two young lads, terrified of the sudden appearance and noise of Alfie, had panicked and tried to dive back in the car, climbing through the open windows *Dukes of Hazzard* style, and not quite making it. Now the dazzling glare of my watchman's torch was in their eyes.

'Down, Alfie,' I bellowed. 'Settle.' He instantly hushed, and I turned my attention to the would-be intruders. 'Who are you, and what the fuck are you doing down here?' I shouted at the lads as they struggled to right themselves into the front seats.

'We're sorry – sorry, man,' one replied. 'We just come down here to smoke by the water. We ain't doing nothing bad.'

They were terrified. Bright-eyed and bushy-tailed in my powerful torch spotlight. I took a photo of the car number plate and one of each of them, shining the beam at their faces in turn.

'This is a private lake,' I told them. 'You can't come down here any more. Next time I'll let him have you.' I pointed at Alfie, knowing he'd never bite anyone, but he convincingly acted the part of a vicious guard dog. And who were they to know he was actually just a big softie?

The lads mumbled more apologies and drove away, never to return. I sent the images the next day to the lake's owner to show I was doing my job, not just swimming in the lake while in hiding. He and I had developed a true friendship born from a mutual respect and a shared sense of humour. It was a glorious isolation in the most beautiful of settings. I was envious of his good fortune, but in a healthy way. He'd earned the place, and he deserved to be happy enjoying it.

But once again I found myself needing an income. I was introduced to a guy who owned a local pub. He was too busy with other work to give the pub the time it needed, and was looking for a live-in landlord. With my previous bar experience it seemed ideal. A way back into normal society. Well, at least a normal house.

After a handshake I moved in and took over the pub. I soon grasped why all the previous managers had left in such quick order. As I enjoyed a honeymoon period and the trade increased, the owner became increasingly irrational and hard to deal with. I'd had to sack a member of staff within weeks of arrival, as she was singly the worst person I'd ever seen behind a bar. Lazy and rude, she spent most of her time trying to seduce any men that came into the pub or offending any women. Her departure was a no-brainer, but it turned out she was also sleeping with the owner. In fact, I was the only member of staff not sleeping with him. I take my beer seriously and regard it as a craft, the whole package. He was just indulging himself with his own drinking hole and a place to shag whoever ended up working behind his bar. So my time there was coming to a hasty end. More and more customers warned me that he was jealous of my success in his pub. That seemed insane to me because surely my success was earning him more money. Anyway, that didn't seem to matter, and we parted on bad terms.

Time to move on again. The lake had been sold, so there was no return to that blissful retreat. It was destined to be a commercial fishing pond surrounded by a huge electric fence to keep otters away from the expensive carp. I was saddened to hear that news: all the animals that visited the lake were now fenced out and that was half the appeal of the place for me.

So, once again, I needed work and somewhere to live. I was lucky to find a job, with digs, in another bar. The owner had run it alone for years, was tired and needed help. We shook hands and I became a fixture. But it was during that year I decided I'd had enough of the pub game. I don't enjoy drunken conversations, especially when I'm the sober one. I needed to start looking further afield, and luckily an old competitor from my Saracen days came in for a drink one night and offered me a job. As simple as that.

And it's going great. I'm back doing what I know best, and things are going well for me again. I had serious misgivings about going out to my old customers: what would their reaction be? I'd pretty much disappeared after losing my business, and wondered if people would want to trust me once more.

Those concerns were groundless, I'm glad to say. It's been nothing but handshakes, cups of tea, and orders placed. I even got a few hugs from normally taciturn engineering managers, genuinely pleased to see me back in the saddle.

During my time in Essex I made contact with an old rugby-team mate who is now a successful author. I initially called him from the cemetery in Colchester while I was filling my water containers, and my chats with him were along the lines of telling my story. The riches to rags, and my topsy-turvy feelings towards the Gypsy way of life, seemed like a tale worth telling. They say that inside every person is one good story. At the time I'd just written some bits of text, extracts from a greater tale with no sense or order to them. I acknowledged that he was sent writing all the time for opinion or review, but I explained my situation and asked him to promise to read mine out of deference to our friendship. He didn't let me down.

About four months ago I found myself passing the plot near Colchester. It was an irresistible pull to go and have a look, and I had no idea what to expect. Would there be people living there again, or would it be empty? I drove up to the gates and could see straight away it was abandoned. Tall grass and weeds had grown around the fence. I climbed over the gate and Alfie comfortably jumped and cleared the five bars, even at eight years old. I watched him run off into the grass, drawing my eye from the gates further into the plot.

My humble trailer, clad in timber to fight the cold, still sat there. Full of memories, good and bad. I walked alongside it and out into the back. The massive lawn I'd mown so regularly was now just a mess of overgrown weeds. I peered through the trailer windows to see the discarded items I'd left behind eighteen months before, sitting exactly where I'd abandoned them. Things that I'd used every day during my time there. Coffee cups and a pen, an empty beer can. The lean-to I'd used to store my firewood still had the discarded generator sitting inside. The bloody thing had never run properly, and I remembered my frustration and despair at trying to start it on a pitch-black winter's night, desperate for some light and television, some comfort in the dark, and pulling the start cord until my fingers bled.

There was no sign that anyone had been there since the day I'd left. Not even Rhoda. It must hurt for her, too.

The only sign of any change were the dozens of new houses that had sprouted up around the plot. Where I'd once enjoyed views of open land there now stood rows of those awful new-build and characterless brick boxes, finished with small, tatty timber porches. So they'd managed to get planning permission after all. Even though my plot had been denied. Purely because it was owned by a Gypsy. It seemed unfair, and my old feelings of resentment at the local authority returned. I whistled for Alfie and we took one last look around. I made a conscious decision I'd never come back. My battles there were long over.

Writing the story of my last eighteen years has been part of a healing process. It's helped me to forgive myself for mistakes I've made, and to put things in perspective. My attitude to a whole community had been wrong: there are good and bad in all walks of life. And were the Gypsies any worse than the bankers or politicians who stole billions and faced no repercussions? Most just wanted to live in a traditional way, unfettered by mortgages and debt. To be given a chance to earn a living with honest graft. Through my toughest times I'd been helped more by those folk than I was by my own community, while facing nothing but barriers and hostility, judgement and prejudice from the system I'd so passionately supported.

If I thought it was in any way possible to live the traditional Romany life in the modern world I'd walk away from regular society tomorrow. But the glory days of Riley and Tillie have passed. Those who remain in the caravans pay a heavy price for their freedom. A price that is demanded by councils and authorities scared of that freedom, afraid of people they can't control.

We're witnessing the last generations of a community outside the modern world, and it'll be all our loss when it has gone for good. I gathered my writings and started to fill in the gaps, wanting to share my experiences as they'd happened, my journey to redemption.

Acknowledgements

With many thanks to Richard Beard, novelist, for connecting the dots; Nicholas Hogg, author, for editing and advising; Charlie Campbell, agent, for believing; and Zennor Compton, editor, for inspiration and advice.